Captain Cook

AND THE SOUTH PACIFIC

The Voyage of the "ENDEAVOUR"

1768–1771

National Maritime Museum, London

The *Endeavour.* "No beauty queen, or greyhound of the seas, but a tough, steady and reliable North Country workman." *From the water colour by Gregory Robinson.*

Captain Cook

AND THE SOUTH PACIFIC

The Voyage of the "Endeavour"

1768–1771

BY

JOHN GWYTHER

ILLUSTRATED

HOUGHTON MIFFLIN COMPANY BOSTON

The Riverside Press Cambridge

LIBRARY OF CONGRESS CATALOGUE CARD NUMBER: 55-6551

PUBLISHED IN ENGLAND AS *First Voyage*

FIRST PUBLISHED IN THE UNITED STATES, 1955

The Riverside Press
CAMBRIDGE • MASSACHUSETTS
PRINTED IN THE U.S.A.

ACKNOWLEDGMENTS

I WOULD LIKE to express my sincere thanks to certain good friends who have assisted me in the writing of this book. Especially to my old friend and former naval colleague, Mr. Kenneth Timings, M.A., for generous advice and criticism given me at all stages of the writing of the book.

To Mr. Gregory Robinson, for keeping a careful eye on the seamanship side of the book and making sure I was not going astern when I should have been going ahead, and for permission to reproduce his splendid painting of the *Endeavour*. Also to his son, Mr. Michael Robinson, Curator of Prints, National Maritime Museum, Greenwich, for help in selecting illustrations. For other illustrations I am indebted to the National Maritime Museum.

Thanks, too, to Mrs. Valerie Enright for deciphering my longhand and assisting with the typing.

Finally to Mr. James Whittaker, F.R.G.S., F.R.H.S., M.I.E.X., for help and advice, sometimes thunderous, quite outside his normal duties as a publisher.

PREFACE

IT ALL started halfway through the morning watch on the 20th of May, 1944. The ship had been sailing north for several days outside the Great Barrier Reef that skirts the eastern coast of Australia and we had gazed with awe at the dreadful coral reefs, for there are literally hundreds of them, some submerged, some just showing and some standing out like jagged teeth, but each one certain destruction to any vessel that ventures too close. They are very beautiful, even to a navigator, and are large horseshoes of shimmering coral, glinting into every dazzling shade of blue, pink and white as the sun plays hide-and-seek amid their naked perfection. Inside the horseshoe the sea is blue — a deep, deep motionless blue as sinister as an unwinking eye.

However, at six o'clock that morning we expected to say good-bye to the Coral Seas and pass through the narrow Endeavour Straits into the Indian Ocean. A dangerous passage, and the Captain had left instructions that he was to be called at 0530. I was second officer of the watch and sent the messenger to shake the Captain. A few minutes later he came stumping on to the bridge, a little puffed from his climb up the steep ladder.

"Morning, pilot."

"Morning, sir," answered the navigator. "We're a little ahead of time; should be up there in about twenty minutes."

The Captain took a look around the horizon, just beginning to grow light.

"Good," he said. "I want an officer in the wheelhouse going through the Straits."

"Aye, aye, sir." The navigator looked at me and followed me to the bridge ladder.

"See what you can do about a cup of char while you're below," he said quietly. "The old man won't be up here long and I can hardly keep my eyes open."

I slithered down the ladder, pushed back the door into the wheelhouse and stepped inside. It had the normal all-night smell of sweat, stale tobacco smoke and strong tea, and the usual quota of sleeping men huddled into the corners for a few minutes down head. I was feeling damn tired myself and not concentrating too well.

"All right, quartermaster?" I asked the man at the wheel, for something to say. "Any hopes of sending the bosun's mate along for a cuppa?"

" 'Sup to you, sir," he answered.

"O.K. then, send him along to the wardroom galley."

I picked up a volume of the *Pilot* — the navigator's Bible — and idly glanced through the instructions for passing through the Straits. The usual stuff: "Masters are advised to keep to the starboard side of the channel, until point something-or-other bears 259 deg." Read on a little farther and sure enough a voice whispers from a hundred and eighty years back: Captain James Cook, "If the wind be blowing from North half East to South, mariners should, etc. . . . By following these instructions I am confident that ships can pass through the Straits without hurt." For a few minutes I watched the helmsman gently spinning the wheel a point or two to starboard, back amidships, then a touch to port, keeping the ship dead on her course. He was a splendidly built man of about thirty, his chest glistening with sweat, and a faint, greenish light from the compass threw weird shadows on his naked body and drew out the bones of his cheeks and brow; round his neck he wore a knotted handkerchief. I noticed how he was half poised on his toes, riding every motion of the ship, his eyes concentrating on the flickering compass needle. The thought struck me that this was a changeless picture; the size of the helm might alter from century to century and it could be turned with a great deal less effort than a hundred years ago; but still, I was watching a scene as old as the hills. The man, the wheel, the compass; and at that moment I could choose to be in whatever year I liked in the history of the sea, for it would still have looked the same.

I thought about Cook. What an extraordinary man he must have been; after over a century and a half he still advised seamen, and accurately, too. In these waters hardly a page of the *Pilot* turned without some reference from him. I remembered an island we had passed a couple of days previously and Cook had told us that "a goodly supply of fresh water may be obtained here, but mariners are warned against the extreme hostility of the natives."

I was finding it hard to keep awake and thoughts were bumping about in my head, jostling each other out of the way. Captain Cook sailed round the world three times and discovered Australia. The famous Duke of York, he had ten

. . . Wonder how you discover a continent? Is it like a pub-crawl when you suddenly find a new public-house, or do you sail away with half a dozen Union Jacks and orders to stick them up here and there about the world? Captain Brown, now what the devil did he do? Played his ukulele as the ship went down. But my mind kept wandering back to Cook; what sort of skipper was he? Had there been a Mrs. Cook and baby Cooks? . . . Tea!

"Quartermaster, what about that cuppa? We're nearly through now."

"Coming up, sir."

How the morning watch dragged on; another hour to go. I'll think about Cook, that will help to keep me awake. And I was telling myself sternly to learn more about him when we got back to England . . .

Then bump! Wake up! I am sitting in front of my own fireplace and it is six years since I kept that weary morning watch; but I did take to heart the ticking off I gave myself about Cook. Since then it has been an absorbing hobby, fitting together like a jigsaw puzzle. The late eighteenth century coming to life before me — the ships, the men, the discipline in the navy of those days, the great unsolved mystery of the South Seas, and the strange mythical continent they believed in, as vast as all the known lands in the Northern Hemisphere; as distant and remote to England then, as Mars is to us today. The colourful history of the Pacific and the heterogeneous collection of adventurers who ventured there before Cook. But above all, Cook, the outstanding personality of his age, and wrapped around him his little ship *Endeavour* and her crew.

To me, sitting in this old farmhouse, built twenty years before Cook was born and sixty years before he discovered Australia, it has become so real that I am going to make the voyage again. Back to the South Seas, and the hundreds of tiny islands, so breathtakingly beautiful, so vividly coloured and set in such blue sea that I cannot even attempt to describe them.

This time I am going back as Cook's private secretary, and rather an idle one at that, for as far as possible I shall let my Captain tell his own story, which he can do far better than I, and enjoy his kindly humour. I shall only fill in the gaps where his modesty prevents his giving a true picture, or where he gets too carried away with his navigational calculations, of which he was very fond.

Therefore I do not claim this as a biography of Cook, but rather as a true yarn of the sea, a story of a voyage that can only be complete when it is humanized by the life they lived aboard, their food, loves, hates, and pleasures, and their reactions to the scenes and dangers as they met them, a story of unflinching courage.

The quotes in this book come from various journals, some are Cook's, some Joseph Banks's, and some are the more moderate words of Dr. Hawkesworth. In a very few cases, in the interests of brevity and clarity, I have done a little paraphrasing, in which I have attempted to maintain the spirit of the original. Within those confines I have striven to be accurate and present Cook's story today with the same impact as it must have had on the reading public in 1773.

But first England, and the navy of about the seventeen-seventies, for great as Cook's achievements were, unless they are set against the typical late eighteenth-century background, his qualities do not stand out as they should and show him as a man years ahead of his time. Yet, he remains a very human person, no doubt with his faults, but these are so few, so far outweighed by his greatness, that it is difficult to be critical.

CONTENTS

ILLUSTRATIONS

Captain Cook

AND THE SOUTH PACIFIC

The Voyage of the "ENDEAVOUR"

1768–1771

I

OAKEN SHIPS AND IRON MASTERS

ENGLAND rigidly divided into classes, the highly cultured landed gentry and noblemen, born to luxury, wealth, and the arts of government, diplomacy, and conversation. The wealthy merchants and great trading houses wherever possible marrying into the outer fringe of the aristocracy. The farmers, the craftsmen, tradesmen, and the bovine mass of labourers. A country united in the certainty of its superiority over every other nation and a belief that no sport was worth while unless blood was let. The golden age of foxhunters, bull-baitings and cockfights, all pastimes which every right-thinking person assured himself brought out the best and manliest qualities in the people.

Happily unaware of the brutality of their age, gentlemen protected their pheasants against poachers with man-traps of a type which today are illegal even for the snaring of vermin. The rich built themselves vast palaces and furnished them with magnificent extravagance, laid out parks and planted great avenues of trees in the certainty that their progeny would enjoy them for ever, and cheerfully gambled away tens of thousands of pounds on the roll of the dice. They ate enormous meals, drank with Bacchanalian abandon, and wed for money and the obligation to breed an heir, for the pleasures of the flesh could be bought cheaply and saved them the necessity of falling in love, a process which only complicated the legal haggling of a marriage settlement.

In London, the coffeehouse was enjoying its heyday and for a few pence men like Boswell and Johnson could idle away a day, debating in their snug warmth. The narrow streets were foul with mud, filth, beggars, ragged children and mongrel dogs. Along the sidewalks apprentices shouted the excellence of their master's wares, swore at their neighbours, and grovelled to the gentry who buried their noses in scented handkerchiefs in a vain attempt to conquer the awful stench of London. Highbred ladies, in the privacy of their sedan chairs, scratched beneath the agonies of their cruel corsets and prepared for the next attack of the vapours. At night it behove one to step warily for there was no lighting and the darkness concealed gangs of cutthroats and thieves willing to go to any lengths for the chance of grabbing a gold watch. Out from the riverside hovels came the whores, snatching at the hat of a passer-by or moaning with false ecstasy in some black alleyway.

A country that waved aside the necessity of a police force and protected its citizens by the legal atrocities of the law; courts which unconcernedly sentenced a lad of eight to death for stealing a pot of paint valued at twopence, or deported for life an eleven-year-old girl who had dressed as a boy and borrowed a neighbour's horse. Every week the prison carts rumbled to the gallows loaded with petty thieves suffering the same extreme penalty as murderers, for hangings were public and served the double purpose of dissuading, by their example, those with criminal intentions and offering free entertainment to the law-abiding citizens. That was the eighteenth-century environment, and accepted as normal, just as today we accept it as normal that a lad in his teens may split open an old woman's skull, rob her and suffer the ignominy of a psychiatrist's examination and a few months' comfortable, corrective training.

But if conditions ashore were harsh they were nothing compared to the crushing servitude that was exacted afloat, especially in the Royal Navy. The great Dr. Johnson considered it a far lesser evil to go to prison than to sea, for the silhouette of the yardarm was the final symbol of the captain's authority. He had the power of life and death and the right to hang a man, and, indeed, hanging was often preferable to some of the frightful punishments that could be meted out. A man seldom survived keel-hauling, and if he did was so horribly mutilated that life could hold little for him. Of all the naval punishments keel-hauling was perhaps the most barbaric. It consisted of dragging the defaulter under the belly of the ship at the broadest point, and the underside of vessels which had been at sea for any length of time were covered with barnacles as sharp and wounding as the broken bottles that are sometimes seen cemented on the tops of walls. If the wretch was lucky he drowned quickly. A dozen lashes of the cat-o'-nine-tails could be awarded for a minor theft and was not placed high in the punishment book. Skilfully applied, so that the thongs flicked into a man's naked back, rather like the action of cracking a whip, each stroke could inflict nine jagged cuts.

Scant medical knowledge approved this method, for a zigzag wound was thought to bleed less than a straight one. Nevertheless, a man who had been flogged wrote this about the punishment: "You hear it coming and it burns. Don't believe what they say about going numb. It burns all the skin off your back, and you feel every stroke."

It might be thought that flogging, keel-hauling and hanging were sufficient deterrents, and one begins to sympathize with Dr. Johnson's point of view. But that is far from the case, and the Admiralty offered several hideous alternatives. Out of thirty-six articles in the list of crimes, ten were punishable by death without option, and a further twelve carried the death penalty at the captain's discretion; if he felt merciful he could choose from one of the following variety: "If any man be convicted of drawing a knife for the purpose of stabbing another or shall have stabbed another, so that blood shall flow, he shall lose a hand." For stealing (and it had to be a piteously small theft to avoid hanging), boiling pitch was poured over the head, and feathers shaken over the culprit to mark him until the ship touched land, when the thief was put ashore, whatever the conditions or lack of the necessities of life might be. The penalty for sleeping on watch if the ship was in enemy waters was to be "beat naked by the crew, and to be plunged into the sea three times with a rope from the yardarm." If a petty officer slept, the punishment was reduced to a starvation ration of dry bread, and a pail of water "thrown over his head downwards."

Murder at sea was quickly dealt with: lash the murderer securely to his dead victim and throw the couple overboard.

And so the list goes on. Ducking, fasting, flogging at the capstan, keel-hauling, or a combination of these tortures.

Hanging weights on offenders "till their heart or back be ready to break" or to "gag or scrape their tongues for blasphemy or swearing." But it must be said in fairness that certain sections of the Navy were beginning to hint that perhaps the punishments were a little too severe and in need of reform. Nevertheless, there they were, to be used or not as the Captain thought fit.

But the British seamen took this punishment like men, silently and in front of the ship's company. Not for a fortune would they utter a murmur or give their tormentors the satisfaction of expressing pain. They stuck it with gritted teeth till they fainted, lashed to the crosstree, to be carried limp and bloody by their shipmates to a berth between decks. The greatest crime was to flinch, for a coward was out, neglected and scorned by his fellows. They came from a race whose very sports were played to the death, and courage, whether in bulldog, cock, horse or prizefighter, was the hallmark of success. There was no room in their age for the timid. You won or you lost, and the loser accepted the penalty, even to death, as just. It was the stakes they played with.

We can read the eyewitness report of a Captain Hammond who watched the hanging of three young sailors sentenced to death for mutiny. He writes:

> On this melancholy occasion, the criminals behaved with great penitence and decorum, acknowledged the justice of their sentence for the crime of which they had been found guilty, and exhorted their fellow sailors to take warning by their untimely fate, and whatever might be their hardships, never to forget their obedience to

their Officers, as a duty they owed to their King and Country.

The Captain adds:

> A party from each ship in the harbour attended the execution, and from reports I have received, the example seems to have made a great impression upon the minds of all the ships' companies present.

A sailor awaiting trial could be clamped in irons and literally left to rot. Midshipman Heywood, who with twelve other seamen survived this treatment, incredible as it may sound, in a letter to his sister described his terrible ordeal:

> A sort of prison was built on the after-part of the quarterdeck into which we were all put in close confinement with both legs and both hands in irons, and were treated with great rigour, not being allowed ever to get out of this den; and, being obliged to eat, drink, sleep and obey the calls of nature here. You may form some idea of the disagreeable situation I must have been in, unable as I was to help myself, (being deprived of the use of both my legs and hands). We slept on nothing but hard boards on wet canvas, without any bed for seventeen months, always subsisting on short allowance of execrable provisions, and without any clothes.

The degree of punishment was left entirely to the discretion of the captain, and some used their authority almost to the point of savagery. Sir John Barrow, who lived about this time, tells us:

> Some few Captains were in the habit of turning over a delinquent to be tried by their messmates, and when found guilty it invariably happened that the punishment inflicted was doubly severe to what it would have been in the ordinary way.

And there is no need to emphasize further the ruthless severity of the "ordinary way."

Sickness, disease, and, above all, scurvy, were rife aboard most ships, and on one summer cruise the *Eagle* buried at sea twenty-two men in a month. On arrival in port she sent a further hundred and thirty of her crew to hospital. How many of those survived we do not know, but it is sufficient to say that a man had to be very ill before a ship's doctor could order any relief from his duties. It was not unusual for a ship which had been at sea for any length of time to lose two-thirds of her crew from sickness. Many of these might have been saved if medical knowledge had not been so atrociously hidebound. Once a man was so obviously ill that he was incapable of carrying on, he was thrust into the most airless part of the vessel aboard: the sick bay. For fresh air, especially at night, was considered the most injurious to recovery of all the elements. This pernicious practice was carried out to such a degree that on one occasion Captain Anson had six air scuttles cut in his ship to prevent the diseased, who were berthed below the waterline, suffocating to death. A further instance of the sketchy hygiene was the gruesome practice of painting the mess decks red to obviate the need of too much scrubbing out or redecorating the ship after she had been in action.

Probably the reason for the high sickness rate was two-fold, and lay partly in damp, poorly ventilated and over-crowded mess decks; the Admiralty's callous answer to high casualties was to carry more men than were needed, for it was a reasonable assumption that a ship would be short-handed before she had been at sea long. Also, the food was atrocious and counted more for the ravages of scurvy than any other factor. Here again the rations were worse than they need have been, for victualling officers found it simple to supplement their pay at the expense of the seamen. But the blame for sickness must be equally shared with the recruiting system. Little, if any, account was taken of the health of men impressed; it was hardly necessary to count their limbs, and in most seaports venereal disease was rife. Consequently ships frequently sailed with a large proportion of their crew unfit, or with symptoms which broke out a few days after leaving harbour.

Captain Anson's unfortunate experience with regard to this side of the question is again worth remembering. He was told to prepare an expedition to the South Seas, but met with considerable difficulties. Instead of receiving able-bodied seamen, he was given a lot of aged, worn-out invalid pensioners of Chelsea College, who had spent the greater part of their lives in the service of their country, but were now herded aboard the ship and perished nearly to a man during this fateful cruise. So many invalids deserted before the ship sailed that at Portsmouth, 210 marines, just recruited and none of whom had yet been taught to fire a gun, were needed to bring the ship's company up to complement.

This was the Navy of Cook's day, which he entered voluntarily. It was enough to brutalize any man, and generally did. To quote Sir John again: "It is indeed a common observation in the Service, that Officers who have risen from before the mast are generally the greatest tyrants." Undoubtedly true, for in later years the infamous "Bligh of the *Bounty*," who served first in the Royal Navy under Cook, and also started on the lower deck, turned into a cruel unreasoning despot, when commissioned, and was described as

> a man of coarse habits, who entertained very mistaken notions with regard to discipline. His temper was irritable in the extreme. In fact he was not a gentleman either by bringing up or by nature. To speak plainly, he was a bully, and not a truthful one. He cursed and swore at his Officers, called them vile names, and accused them without proof or reason of discreditable offences.

Cook could not have been blamed if he had travelled in that direction, too; instead, he saw the badness, the unnecessary cruelty, and the suffering caused to the sailors by neglect and inexperience, and when authority came to him he did not exact the proverbial eye for an eye, but threw all his energies into righting these obvious wrongs and still maintained discipline. In this, above all else, lay his greatness.

II

THE FARMER'S BOY GOES TO SEA

1728–1767

TOWARDS dusk on the 27th of October, 1728, in the village of Marton, Yorkshire, Grace Cook was safely delivered of a son, a thing of no great importance to anybody, not even Grace, who yearly bore her husband a child and looked upon it as the most unpleasant and painful of the calendar's anniversaries. She had had nine children; this child, James, was the seventh, or perhaps the sixth. Grace found it difficult to remember; the christening of one child heralded the conception of another. In her life there was no time for self-pity. A life of unending work, as her mother's had been and her grandmother's before that, as was her husband's on the farm. Sowing, lambing, harvest, ploughing — unending and unchanging. The sow had two litters a year and she had a child. One just went on, working hard and honestly, grateful for the mud cottage and a bellyful of grub.

Two years after the birth of James, however, a great change came to the Cooks; their years of stubborn work were rewarded with a rise in both income and status. Mr. Scottowe, their employer, made Cook his bailiff at a large farm in Ayrton, about four miles away. Life was a little easier, but still the seasons remained their unrelenting master, until one day, several years later, when Mr. Scottowe noticed the family again and in particular James. The boy showed promise, he must be sent to the village school to see whether Mistress Mary Walker could instruct him in the rudiments of writing and arithmetic. In this she had little difficulty, for "he soon displayed a very early genius for figures," and quickly absorbed the limited teaching she could give him. And so back to the farm to work with his father, no doubt with the intention that one day he would take over from him; but this was not to be.

When James was about seventeen his parents decided that their son had the exact qualifications to enter the general grocery trade. He was a hard-working lad, perhaps a little over-fond of reading, but good at his figures. Accordingly, young Cook kicked the earth from his boots, but could not shake it from his soul.

The road to the grocer's shop led directly to the sea, and Cook was apprenticed to a Mr. Sanderson at Staithes on the Yorkshire coast. Here he slept under the counter by night and worked under the threat of the stick by day. His very limited spare time was spent down at the tiny harbour, for seamen and ships had begun to entrance his mind and thoughts. He could never tire of listening to their stories of hardship and danger, and every detail was of interest to him. Always questioning, sometimes he got a right answer, but more often than not a kick, and he would creep back up the hill to his draughty bunk under the counter, his ears stinging with the last drunken cuff and the sound of their mocking laughter: "Bloody boy'll never make a seaman, damme, he stands over six foot, how the hell's 'e going to get about 'tween decks." Rough, tough men, drinking and wenching their only pastimes; tempers as fiery as the rum they drank; bodies as hard as the oak of their ship, and lusts as coarse as the weevily rations they fed on. But the finest seamen in the world.

Lying sleepless at night with the roar of the surf in his ears, young James's thoughts were always of the sea. A resolution began to build in his mind that ships, not shops, were his life. A resolve that grew and could not be resisted. He had to get away. Cook thought all round his problem. He had been with Mr. Sanderson barely a year, and that left another two of his intolerable apprenticeship.

He would, and must, ask Mr. Sanderson to release him. This was not a rushed decision, no stealing a shilling from the till and boarding the first ship he could find, for the sea was going to be his life and James Cook meant that career to be a success. Then he would start right, with the blessings of his old master and his family, not their curses. Who knows what a good word from his employer might not do?

Mr. Sanderson had also been doing some thinking and had arrived at precisely the same conclusions as James. He had no complaints about the boy, he worked hard, but it was quite evident that he had not the reverence for sultanas and salt that would make a successful general grocer, and so, when James approached him, after a ponderous and dignified two days of agonizing silence for his apprentice, Mr. Sanderson gave his consent. Even better, he had a ship-owning acquaintance in Whitby who had a small fleet of coal boats. He would write to Mr. Walker and see what he could arrange for his young friend. This was all and more than Cook had hoped for, especially when consent was received from Mr. Walker.

Cook travelled to Whitby to join his first ship, the *Freelove,* a collier of about 450 tons. He was immediately conspicuous, but unfortunately not as he wanted to be. His height for one thing — he stood over six feet — and at eighteen he was at least three or four years older than the usual starting age of an apprentice; shipmates of his own years were experienced seamen. So far as James was concerned these were minor setbacks, for at least he was part of a ship and no longer a boy standing on the quayside, gazing and longing. He felt almost as though he owned the *Freelove* and admired every inch of her. But he soon learned that the sailors' talk he had listened to back at Staithes was not exaggerated. Life on a collier for an apprentice was hard and uncomfortable. His best was not always good enough, and the rope's end, laid on with a liberal hand, was the finest way known to make a seaman. There was no particular system about these lashings, their administration depended solely on his superior's liver, and Cook was the most junior hand aboard. A look was enough to warrant a stunning kick from a heavy sea boot, and there was no reprisal. Discipline was hard and often unnecessarily cruel, and crew were worked almost to exhaustion in all weathers and at all hours. Their living quarters were dark, damp and overcrowded. When the collier was loaded and lying low in the water, a grey mess of sea water, mixed with coal dust, continually sloshed around their ankles as they worked, or sat in the mess deck chewing the filthy mixtures that were served up as food.

Far from being deterred by the conditions, young Cook

was indefatigable in his efforts to master his trade. He soon realized that coal boats and the east coast of England combined to give a man one of the finest groundings in seamanship imaginable. The coast abounded with shoals and shallows and the harbours were mostly tidal. Masters of ships needed as great a skill in pilotage as navigation to sail their vessels safely. The coal boats themselves were fine examples of the skill of British shipbuilders, for they had to be exceptionally strongly made to withstand grounding when fully loaded. By no means fast vessels or comfortable sea boats, their qualities lay in their great strength and shallow draft — qualities which Cook was to remember and utilize to the utmost in later years.

For three years he served his apprenticeship in these vessels, mostly coaling, but with occasional voyages to Norway and the Netherlands and a spell in the dockyards, assisting in the rigging and fitting out of a new 600-ton vessel, the *Three Brothers*.

Mr. Walker quickly realized that he had an apprentice of exceptional ability and diligence, for there was some inexplicable quality about James Cook that immediately impressed itself on his seniors, a great capacity to concentrate and hang on to a subject until he had mastered it; he had the clear, sharp brain of a realist and mathematician. A young man who learned from lessons and experiences stepped confidently into the future on assumption of his own, which generally proved correct.

At the end of his apprenticeship, Cook decided that he would learn more by joining another company. This he did, and for the next three years he sailed for several different owners as an able seaman. Now, at the age of twenty-five, came his first real step forward. He re-entered the service of his old friend Mr. Walker, who made him mate of one of his ships, the *Friendship*. It was rapid promotion, to rise in six years from an apprentice, born and bred from generations of landsmen, to mate of a seagoing ship.

All this time the international contest for sea power and colonies which had been going on spasmodically since 1739 formed a lively background to Cook's first years at sea, and finally, in 1744, merged into a full-scale war with France. The Royal Navy was in a shocking state of repair, ships that had been laid up for years were badly in need of overhauls, and personnel were down to about a quarter of the country's requirements. The Navy was placed on a war footing, and in every port and harbour the dreaded press gangs were ruthlessly at work. This was all before Cook's eyes and must have formed the chief topic of conversation between sailors of every description. Too often had he seen men dragged from the quayside taverns, drunk or sober, their screaming wives and wenches fighting hysterically to release the prisoners. They wept for their men, whose chances of returning to them, even maimed, were remote.

Cook himself was not in any danger of being impressed, especially as Mr. Walker had recently offered to make him captain of one of his vessels. He was twenty-seven, and after only eight years of the sea, at the top of his profession, with an assured future, good salary and as much comfort as anyone had in a hard career. In addition, he was his own master, responsible to one man only, his employer, who, it is certain, had the greatest faith in his future captain.

At this stage James Cook made the most important and vital decision of his life. He determined to join the Royal Navy. But there was only one way in for a man of his humble birth: right at the bottom as an able seaman. Once embarked on that road, there was no turning back; gone would be his position of authority, his captaincy and comfortable salary. It meant starting again. But Cook had carefully weighed his chances. The Navy was crammed to bursting point with untrained, raw, impressed recruits, and new ships were being commissioned every day. Surely there must be opportunities for a man of his calibre to rise quickly, for he was convinced in his own mind that his considerable qualities would soon be noticed and lead to promotion. As he himself said, "I had a mind to try my fortune that way."

So Cook travelled to London and on June 17, 1755, entered the King's Service. A week later he was sent to Portsmouth and joined His Majesty's Ship *Eagle,* a 60-gunner.

When Cook joined the *Eagle* she was commanded by Captain Hamer. It took that gentleman little over a month to spot his outstanding abilities, and James was promoted to Master's Mate. Hamer was shortly superseded by Captain Hugh Palliser, and again within two months of the appointment Cook's qualities were obvious to this new captain. Promotion followed to Boatswain, in a ship the size of the *Eagle* quite a responsible position.

During this period the *Eagle* assisted in the blockade of the French coast, an exacting duty with little to break the monotony of endless months of cruising in the Channel, often with the coast of England in sight. So far as the ship's company were concerned, their homeland might have been a thousand miles away. But in all weathers, the British navy prowled like a cat waiting to pounce on any French mouse that dared to show itself from the enemy coast. H.M.S. *Eagle* took several prizes. Cook had risen so far in the estimation of Captain Palliser that on one occasion he was put in command of a large prize ship, which he brought successfully into the Thames. They had one bloody engagement with a Frenchman, which cost the *Eagle* forty-two lives; still a lesser number than they suffered from sickness.

By now it had become apparent to everybody connected with Cook that his merits deserved greater recognition, and Captain Palliser recommended him to the Admiralty for a commission. This was backed up by a letter from his old friend Mr. Walker, and another, which, at the request of several of his friends and neighbours, was written for him by Mr. Osbaldiston, M.P. for Scarborough.

For a long time past it had been the custom that a gentleman's promotion was influenced chiefly by the length of his pedigree or the lofty connection of his friends, little attention being paid to his qualities as a naval officer. The results had sometimes been appalling; mere boys were appointed to positions of authority which they were quite incapable of filling. It took the Admiralty several centuries to learn its lesson, but unfortunately for Cook, they did, just about the time that he was recommended for promotion. A new ruling was approved which laid down that a man must serve six years with the Royal Navy before he could receive the King's Commission. That gave Cook another four years to wait. It was unfair to the really brilliant man and made practically no difference to a well-bred slacker who could easily be found a cosy job ashore for his first six years in the service.

Instead of his commission, Cook was given a Master's warrant, and the Admiralty, with meritorious efficiency, sent him first to a sloop, but overlooked the fact that the ship already had a perfectly adequate master. Secondly the Admiralty sent him to H.M.S. *Garland,* forgetting that they had ordered the vessel to sea some days previously; but finally, after a short spell aboard the *Soleby,* he was made Master of the *Pembroke,* a 64-gun ship of the line.

The Master of one of His Majesty's ships held a peculiarly responsible position. He was firstly a warrant officer and could only rise to that rank from the lower deck. This was important because, not only had he to pass on orders from his senior officers, but, if necessary — and it frequently was — show a sailor how to carry out that order. The Master, therefore, acted as liaison officer between the lower deck and the quarter-deck. In addition, he was responsible for the general running of the ship, and most important of all, navigation and pilotage. The latter two subjects were a closed book to the sailors, and not very wide open to quite a number of officers. It is probably true to say that though not second in seniority to the Captain, the Master was next in importance to him. Certainly his loss would be a far greater disaster to any ship than the disappearance of half a dozen junior officers. A further pointer to his standing was that it would be a most unusual event for the Captain and his Master to be off the ship at the same time. He had to be a complete mariner, both in the practice and theory of seamanship.

In 1758 the *Pembroke* joined the fleet which conveyed Wolfe and Amherst to North America. One of her first duties was to assist in the successful siege of Louisburg, whose destruction was essential before Wolfe could attempt the assault of Quebec.

It was fifty years since the English had tried to regain Quebec, and that operation had been a costly failure, with many fine ships wrecked and about 800 lives lost on the treacherous reefs of the St. Lawrence estuary. Wolfe rightly came to the decision that no landing could be contemplated until the approaches to Quebec were accurately charted. The men selected for this duty were the Masters of His Majesty's ships, which included Cook, with their expert knowledge of pilotage and handling of small boats.

It was desperately dangerous work and could only be carried out on the blackest of nights. Paddling noiselessly, with muffled rowlocks in utter darkness, among unknown waters, each night they came to the actual landing places, and closer to the shore batteries of the French. If the moon were to break through, their boats would stand out on the shimmering moonlit water like ink blots on a clean sheet; sitting targets for the French shore guns. There was the ever present danger of fire ships and enemy skirmishing parties or canoe loads of hostile Indians gliding stealthily amid the shoals searching for the fine trophy of an English scalp. Indeed, they got so close to Cook one night that he only managed to escape over the bows of his boat as the Indians clambered over the stern.

Despite the appalling dangers and difficulties, the warrant officers of the Royal Navy made a superb job of their surveying, without which it is doubtful if the assault on Quebec could have been attempted. And it seems reasonable to suppose that Cook was the most skilful and senior among them, for he alone was personally consulted by General Wolfe before the offensive, on the approach to the landing places. Further, he was quite unofficially referred to as "Master of the Fleet" and "Master Surveyor." Why? Because Cook always learned to qualify himself, to do something more than the ordinary routine of his duty.

Quebec fell in 1759 and the majority of the British fleet were sent home, but Cook was almost certainly retained as Master of Lord Colville's flagship, the *Northumberland,* to continue the survey of the coast and estuaries of North America. As ever, the work he did was superb and his charts were considered among the finest surveys ever made, and superseded all others of the period for accuracy. Many of them were published. But his routine work was not enough for him, and all his leisure hours were devoted to further study. "It is here, as I have often heard him say," writes Captain King, his friend, pupil and fellow explorer, "that, during a hard winter, he first read Euclid, and applied himself to the study of mathematics and astronomy, without any other assistance than that afforded by a few books and his own industry."

Cook's brilliance did not pass unnoticed and successive commanders liked and respected the man. Sir Charles Saunders, Lord Colville, Sir Edward Hawke, Admiral Graves, and Sir Hugh Palliser were all deeply impressed by his brilliance, and "continued to patronize him during the rest of their lives with the greatest zeal and affection."

His qualities seeped through, even to the Admiralty, who began to realize that in Cook they had a servant of "Genius and capacity . . . for undertakings of the same kind."

In 1762 the *Northumberland* was ordered home and reached England in November of that year. James Cook was still without a commission, probably at his own wish, for he had served well over the qualifying six years, and his record, together with the recommendation he could expect, was more than sufficient to advance him to the wardroom. Perhaps he continued to remain an uncommissioned mate for financial reasons; the messing would certainly be cheaper, or maybe the individuality of his position aboard suited him better. Possibly the company in the warrant officers' mess was more to his liking, men of his own standing who had started at the bottom and risen only through their own initiative. He may have felt diffident about mixing with the young commissioned gentlemen, for to the end of his days he remained reticent about his early life, and England in the eighteenth century was class-conscious.

About a month after arriving home, Cook married Elizabeth Batts, who belonged to a family of tradesmen dwelling about the Thames waterside. He was now thirty-four and his bride twenty-one. They were married at Shadwell and later moved to a house in Mile End.

At first appearances it looks like love at first sight, and if so, was about the only unpremeditated action Cook ever took in his life. Nor was it consistent with the essentially practical outlook of his century, when marriages were arranged and a careful eye was kept on the financial side of the union, for love was believed to blossom better to its fullness on a firm foundation of English sterling. Let us believe he had known Elizabeth since she was a child and was, in fact, her godfather, and at that ceremony he had "declared his wish for their future union." Whatever the truth may be, Providence and My Lords of the Admiralty looked kindly on the marriage. Cook returned to his surveying in North America, but thanks to his old friend Sir Hugh Palliser, now Governor of Newfoundland, James was given his own schooner, the *Grenville*. In this he surveyed the coasts during the summer months and returned to England in the winter to work on his charts and put his wife in the family way, with a regularity as great and accurate as the new chronometer just being perfected by John Harrison. No doubt his admiration was equal both for the chronometer as a fine aid to navigation and for his wife, who faithfully carried out the main function of an eighteenth-century marriage by bearing him children.

It is sad to relate that with the exception of those first few years, Mrs. Cook saw little of her husband, and the news of his death was followed by a string of tragedies for her.

A pension of £200 per annum was settled by the King on Cook's widow, and £25 per annum on each of his three children, none of whom long survived him. Nathaniel, the second son, a midshipman on board the *Thunderer,* was lost with that vessel, which foundered at sea; he was then only sixteen years old. Hugh, the youngest child, who was a student at Christ College, Cambridge, died there at the age of seventeen; and in the next year, James, the eldest son, then commander of the *Spitfire,* sloop of war, was drowned in his thirty-second year with his boat's whole crew off the

Isle of Wight. A daughter had previously died of dropsy when about twelve years of age. Thus a few short years saw the widow of the great navigator left alone in the world, bereft of all the ties which were most dear to her. She long survived; but always observed the four sad anniversaries, on each recurrence of which she was accustomed to seclude herself, and give up her thoughts to the memory of the dead. She had fixed her residence at Clapham, so that she might enjoy the company of her son James, whenever his duties called him to London, and there she continued to reside until death at length called her, in her ninety-fourth year. Her circumstances, independently of her pension, were easy, and she left large sums to various charities. Her most precious relic, the Copley medal, which had been voted to her husband for his improved method of preserving the health of seamen during long voyages, and which he did not live to receive, she bequeathed to the British Museum.

While on the *Grenville* Cook was paid the comfortable salary of ten shillings a day and given the unusual title of "Mr. J. Cook, Engineer" and again as "King's Surveyor," all indications of his singular ability and high standing with the Admiralty. His duties did not finish with surveying; the hard-learned lessons of astronomy were utilized. A paper he wrote, entitled "An Observation of an Eclipse of the Sun at the Island of Newfoundland," was published by the Royal Society in their *Philosophical Transactions* — certainly a great honour.

The raw young farmer's boy had come a long way from the cloying Yorkshire mud, under the grocer's counter, by the kicks and curses of the Merchant Service, the hell and disease of the Royal Navy, to be recognized as a great, practical seaman, a superb navigator and pilot of unquestioned courage and a brilliant mathematician, described by the Royal Society as "Mr. Cook, a good mathematician, very expert in his business." Ten words, equal to an honours' degree today. He could count among his friends a dozen highly placed and titled people in the country, and the secret was unrelenting hard work, self-teaching, self-reliance, bravery and modesty.

III

THE SHIP AND HER COMPANY

December, 1767 – August, 1768

COOK brought his little ship *Grenville* back to England for the winter of 1767–68, and before him lay his usual task of working up and presenting his charts to the Admiralty and preparing his vessel for the next spring's surveying on the North American coast. A pleasant routine with the prospect of Christmas at home with his wife and family.

But as the bright yellow spokes of the stagecoach wheels were merged into one pattern while they dashed breathtakingly about the English highways at fifteen miles an hour, so the many circumstances that were to send Cook on his next commission were confused; and until the wheel stops we cannot tell that the pattern is made up of all the spokes, pointing to a hub, on the centre of which is written "Cook."

One spoke goes back as far as 1639, when Jeremiah Horricks, an astronomer, observed from Lancashire the transit of Venus across the face of the sun. That phenomenon had not been seen since, but early in the eighteenth century the Astronomer Royal, Edmund Halley, calculated that it would occur again probably in 1769. The forthcoming transit was of interest to the whole scientific world. The Royal Society considered the observation so important (it was hoped the results would assist in ascertaining longitude by lunar observation) that they appointed a committee to go into the question. Those learned gentlemen spent many an hour in profound and wordy debate, until the combined efforts of their nodding heads, weighed down by the colossal amount of brain, reported to the Royal Society that the observation could best be made from points in Norway, the Hudson Bay and the mysterious, little-known South Pacific.

Norway and the Hudson Bay presented little difficulty, but the South Pacific, that was a different question, involving a long and hazardous sea voyage. Undeterred, the Society approached their patron, King George III, and asked for his assistance in furnishing a vessel for the expedition. They went hopefully, for their king was sympathetic to all the arts of science, and had already sent two expeditions to the Pacific, one of which, under Wallis and Carteret, was still at sea. They were not disappointed. His Majesty graciously promised them £4000 and a suitable ship to be prepared by the Royal Navy. On the 29th of February, 1768, Lord Shelbourne, Secretary of State, formally notified the Admiralty that they were to provide a ship for a Pacific expedition.

The Royal Society hoped to combine the observation with an exploration of the South Pacific seas, for it was generally believed among geographers that the Southern Hemisphere contained a large lump of land. This unknown continent was shown on their maps, stretching unbroken from the tip of South America, right across the Pacific to latitude 160° west. It was a vast country, quite as big as Europe and Asia combined, and labelled "Terra Australis Nondum Cognita." The arguments for its existence were that there must be this equivalent amount of land in the Southern Hemisphere to counteract the weight of that in the Northern, and so keep the world on an even keel. They also hoped that besides appointing the scientific staff they would be allowed to incorporate one of their own team as commander of the expedition; it would not have been a precedent. Moreover, they believed they had the ideal man for the position, Dalrymple. And that gentleman was even more convinced than the Society that he was positively the only leader that any sane person could think of, as being fit to command so important a voyage. The observations of Venus were of secondary importance to Dalrymple. His real ambition lay in being the discoverer of the mighty Southern Continent, in which he was a firm and unshakable believer. The prospect was enough to fire enthusiasm in any ambitious man.

In all fairness, Dalrymple was not wholly unsuited for the post. He had a certain amount of practical seamanship, could navigate and had done some surveying for the East India Company. Scientifically he was well fitted, for he was a sound botanist and astrologer, and a member of the Royal Society, who strongly backed his claims, as did also the Astronomer Royal. In addition, he had read widely and probably knew as much about the South Pacific as was known to anybody at that time.

There was just one small point which the Royal Society and Dalrymple had overlooked, the Navy. They were to supply the ship, and by Heaven, they would supply its commander; the two were one in their mind. At a stormy meeting the First Lord of the Admiralty crashed his fist on the table and shouted in their astonished faces that he would rather lose his right hand than entrust one of His Majesty's ships to a man who was not in the Navy. The scientific gentlemen bowed, called for their carriage, and retreated to the safety of their musty archives.

The Admiralty had good reasons for insisting that the commander of the expedition should be an officer in the Navy. They were as keen as the Royal Society to combine the observation with a voyage of discovery, but this was kept secret from the Society. The Navy's mind was more open and alert to foreign affairs. They were not so concerned with balancing the world geographically as to establishing once and for all, the existence or non-existence of the Southern Continent. If it did exist, then it was important to the security of Great Britain to get there first before any monkeying Frenchman or Spaniard had the same idea. In addition, the new lands, always supposing there were any, might contain considerable natural wealth, and that, too, would be far better placed in British pockets.

Besides, this business of combining scientist and commander had been tried before. Edmund Halley was made a temporary captain to command a scientific expedition, but a mutiny in his ship rather inclined their lordships to the belief that star-gazing and discipline were in no way connected. Dampier, another seagoing civilian, had succeeded little better, and on his return from a voyage was court-martialled and found guilty of ill-treating his first lieutenant and declared unfit to command. In any case the regulation was still in force that a man must serve six years before he could be commissioned. All these reasons might have been overcome had not Dalrymple been a boastful, conceited and unpleasant creature, overconscious of his own greatness. My Lords of the Admiralty did not like him and that was just as sufficient a reason then as it is today to strike their quill through his name, sprinkle the sand and forget the matter.

The choice of a commander was of vital importance, and the Admiralty considered several names. Finally, on the advice of Mr. Stephenson, Secretary to the Admiralty, and a strong recommendation from Sir Hugh Palliser, now well advanced in the Service, Cook was chosen. Whether or not he had any idea of what was coming is a matter of pure speculation, but it does seem reasonably certain that when he returned home that winter from North America, he had not the least idea of, or interest in a voyage to the South Seas. So it must have come as a considerable surprise to Cook when their lordships requested his presence and informed him that he was to be commissioned Lieutenant to command a ship on a voyage of discovery.

As Cook left the Admiralty, the tremendous fact struck him. He was well aware of the dangers and hardships that were inseparable from such a voyage into the unknown. Imagine a warrant officer in the Royal Air Force today being told that he was commissioned and must immediately prepare an expedition to the moon. Even that is not a true comparison, for today's explorer does know there is a moon, well photographed. Cook was to sail into an unknown, uncharted void, to discover an imaginary continent as large as the whole world, so the experts said. And their imagination did not stop there, for they peopled their mythical lands with giants and frightful monsters. Yet Cook was not alarmed, his mind was free of superstition and open only to the business of preparing himself, his ship and her crew to face whatever danger might lie before them.

Needless to say, Dalrymple's spite and rancour were intense when he learned that the command of the expedition had been given to a comparatively unknown, ill-bred warrant officer. The Royal Society implored him to go as head of the scientific staff, but it was more than his overblown pride could stand to play second fiddle to any man, least of all a jumped-up able seaman. One thing only can be said in his favour, he did overcome his dreadful bitterness sufficiently before the expedition sailed to give Joseph Banks, head of the scientific staff, a secret document he discovered in Madras, in which Luis Vaez de Torres claimed to have sailed between New Guinea and north Australia — the strait now known as Torres Strait. It is significant that he gave this paper to Banks. Nothing on earth would have induced him to have any direct, contaminating contact with Cook, whom he considered immeasurably his inferior. Even after the successful circumnavigation of the world by Cook, Dalrymple did his utmost to belittle the achievement and made direct attacks on Cook's integrity.

The Admiralty had named their man, it now remained to supply him with a suitable ship, and after inspecting a number of vessels the Navy Board finally selected a sturdy little Yorkshireman, in fact a Whitby collier, the same type of ship that Cook had first gone to sea in. Her original name was the *Earl of Pembroke,* but this was changed to the more suitable name of *Endeavour.* She was a roomy, bluff-bowed vessel of 370 tons, with an overall length of 105 feet and a 29-

foot beam, square-sterned and, like all the coal boats, very strongly built, with shallow draft and ample space for stowage of stores. The *Endeavour* was no beauty queen, or greyhound of the seas, but a tough, steady and reliable North Country workman. She carried ten carriage and twelve swivel guns, exceptionally light armament; but she sailed with no warlike intentions, so it was unnecessary to clutter up her decks and valuable stowage space with cannon.

Considerable alterations and repairs were done to her. The Admiralty spent with a generous hand, paying almost as much on improvements as the cost of purchasing the ship — a precedent for those days, but an indication of the importance that was attached to the forthcoming voyage. Her bottom was given an extra skin, sandwiched between which and the ship's side was tarred felt as a precaution against worms in tropical waters. Cook preferred this expedient to sheathing the ship below the waterline with copper, which he feared might be too easily torn off on shoals.

With a justifiable pride, Cook wrote: "Having received my Commission, which was dated the 25th of May 1768, I went on board on the 27th, hoisted the pennant, and took charge of the ship, which then lay in the basin in Deptford yard." He was forty at the time.

Whatever may be argued, it is almost too much of a coincidence to believe that Cook did not have some influence in the choice of a Whitby collier, for it seems certain that if the selection had been left to him alone she is the ship he would have chosen. In any case, Cook's and the Navy Board's description of her good points are so much akin that it may be assumed that as the port circled the table, Cook and those worthy gentlemen had indeed discussed her choice. For Cook pointed out the type of vessel he thought best suited to exploration. He says:

> A ship of this kind must not be of a great draft of water, yet of sufficient burden and capacity to carry a proper quantity of provisions and necessaries for her complement of men, and for the term requisite to perform her voyage. She must also be of a construction that will bear to take the ground, and of a size which, in case of necessity, may be safely and conveniently laid on shore, to repair any accidental damage or defect. These properties are not to be found in ships of war of forty guns, nor in frigates, nor in East India Company ships, nor in large three-decked West India ships, nor, indeed, in any other but North country ships such as are built for the coal trade, which are peculiarly adapted for this purpose.

The Navy Board go on to recommend a vessel to the Admiralty in these words: "Your Lordships might consider a cat-built vessel [meaning a collier], a type which are roomy and will afford the advantage of stowing and carrying a large quantity of provisions so necessary on such voyages, and in this respect, preferable to ships of war."

The ship's company were carefully chosen and included, greatly to Cook's satisfaction, several seamen just returned from Wallis' Pacific voyage. The principal members were Lieutenant Zachary Hicks, First Lieutenant, or "Jimmy the One," an experienced seaman but apt to be a little "trigger happy" with the natives when his commander was not aboard; Lieutenant John Gore, a well-seasoned sailor who had survived already two circumnavigations of the world; Robert Molineux, the Master, and his two mates, Richard Pickersgill and Charles Clarke, all three of whom had been with Captain Wallis; Mr. Monkhouse, the surgeon, and John Satterly, the carpenter, rather ominously linked together. Perhaps an exchange of tools would be necessary. Each had a mate: Stephen Forward, the gunner, and Richard Orton, clerk. The rest of the crew consisted of a cook, a steward, two quartermasters, an armourer, sailmaker and three midshipmen (one of whom, James Matra, had the most barbaric notions of a practical joke, as will be seen later, and was not a particularly good influence on the other two "snotties"), forty-one able seamen, twelve marines, and nine servants.

Meanwhile the Royal Society had selected its team, a little overpowering in size as far as Cook and the Navy were concerned.

The most colourful member of the civilian party was undoubtedly Joseph Banks, a huge, immensely tough, likable young man of twenty-five. The Royal Society still preserves a great chair, specially made to accommodate his muscular bulk. Mr. Banks, later Sir Joseph, was an extremely wealthy and well-connected gentleman; it was partly his friendship with Lord Sandwich, the First Lord of the Admiralty, that earned him his place in the team. High-spirited and impetuous, at times almost to the point of stupidity, he must have sorely tried the patience of the methodical Cook on more than one occasion. He came as a botanist, in which capacity he was quite brilliant, but his curiosity was insatiable and everything, whether it were a half-rotten and highly scented corpse, or a beautiful and very much alive Tahitan princess, was investigated to the full. He also developed quite a flair for trading and dealing with the natives. Typical of the man is a remark he made when advised to go on the fashionable Grand Tour of Europe: "Every blockhead does that, my grand tour shall be round the world." It needed a man with the firmness and character of Cook to keep Banks in his place, but it is to the credit of both that — despite their widely different upbringing and birth — Cook's authority as Captain was never questioned or undermined. The mutual respect and liking which grew between them lasted a lifetime.

Banks brought a team to assist with his botanical research and paid his own and their expenses throughout the voyage. Dr. Solander, his second-in-command, was a librarian from the British Museum, and an enthusiastic and knowledgeable student of natural history, unfortunately rather more prone to preach than to practise, a characteristic which, but for the bravery of Banks, would have cost him his life in the frozen mountains of South America early in the voyage. There were also Alexander Buchan and Sidney Parkinson, two artists engaged to sketch views and plants; and two Negro servants.

The Royal Society nominated Charles Green, assistant to the Astronomer Royal, as one of the observers, and so impressed were they at their first personal meeting with Cook and by the knowledge of the splendid work he had already done that they appointed him the other observer. In addition, the Society paid him a considerable fee and supplied his instruments.

During this period of selection and rejection, recommendations, commissions, warrants, all the mass of paper and flurrying of harried, ink-stained clerks, the *Endeavour* was working hard. Each day the piles of stores grew greater on the dockside at Deptford, and apparent confusion reigned. The separate heads of departments aboard, each certain that his own personal problems of stowage was the greatest, overwhelmed the First Lieutenant, Mr. Hicks, who was desperately trying to satisfy their incessant demands, cajolings, threats and beggings for bigger working parties. Stores put in the wrong place, stores lost, stores broken. Poor Jimmy the One, he must have scratched his head in dismay mingled with disgust at the mountainous heaps of scientific paraphernalia, boxes for butterflies, tins for specimens, lenses for God knows what, books and atlases, attended by undisciplined, fussing civilians who flung up their arms in distress as the sailors cheerfully tossed about their precious instruments with the contempt they deserved. Jack couldn't care less. But Lieutenants Hicks and Gore could smile grimly to each other — just wait till they got this bunch of landlubbers at sea. They thought gleefully of the effects of salted, fat pork, followed by a freshening wind beating the sea into a choppy swell. That would sort out this mob and change their twittering to groans. Ah, yes! The thought pleased and sustained them.

And behind it all, Cook, quietly checking details and busying himself with his main concern, the health of his crew when they got to sea, for disease and scurvy were relentless, ever present enemies that could wipe out his ship's company. He had only to think back to Commodore Anson's last horrifying voyage, when at one point he was losing five to six men daily: April, forty-three dead from scurvy; May, another eighty dead; and by June only two hundred men left from a crew of nearly five hundred. Cook intended to fight this menace with three main weapons. Firstly, every known antiscorbutic medicine was taken aboard, and Cook listed them thus: "We had besides many extra articles such as malt, saurkraut, salted cabbage, portable broth, saloup, mustard, marmalade of carrot and inspissated juice of wort, and beer." Some of them sound nasty enough to be effective, especially when we read the further instructions, "from one to five or six pints a day as the surgeon sees necessary." Secondly, Cook was meticulously careful about the cleanliness of his ship and the personal hygiene of the sailors. He never missed an opportunity to scrub out and fumigate the mess decks. To ensure still further the health of his crew, sufficient extra warm clothing was carried to make certain that no man need work or sleep in damp garments. His third rule was to change the drinking water and embark fresh meat and vegetables whenever possible.

Quite a few of these precautions were common usage in the Navy, but where Cook differed from the majority of sea captains was in his strict enforcement of the methods, even reverting to the lash to make sure a man took his daily dose. The proof of the pudding was in the eating: for the first time in the recorded history of a long sea voyage, not one man was lost from scurvy.

Gradually the chaos above and below decks began to right itself. The piles of stores on the dockside slowly diminished as *Endeavour* noisily digested them and the smiles of Lieutenants Hicks and Gore became more grim and knowing as their day approached. Finally all was stowed away and the bosun's pipe trilled shrilly above the din of the dockyard: "Special sea-duty men to your stations, mast-head men away aloft."

Quietly *Endeavour* slipped out into the Thames. "Stores and provisions having been taken on board, sailed down the river on the 30th June and on the 13th August anchored in Plymouth Sound," writes Cook.

Here Banks and his party joined the ship, and the crew were delighted to receive two months' wages in advance, despite the fact that they were told they were to expect no additional pay for the remainder of the voyage.

"While we lay here waiting for a wind, the articles of War and the Act of Parliament were read to the ship's company." Cook addressed his crew, a little ceremony carried out as long as ships have sailed the seas, a few gruff words, themselves meaning little but the action of the captain looking over his ship's company and allowing them to size him up for the first time contains all the deep-rooted traditions of the sea. From the moment a man is made captain of a vessel, he and his ship are one. It is the marriage of captain and ship to the crew. Looking down on his men, Cook would see a pattern of upturned faces, scarcely known to him, but each of whose lives was in his hand. None could be allowed for a second to be stronger than himself, for whatever dangers faced them ahead his men must never detect a trace of indecision or fear in his manner. From now on, Cook's life training and every fibre of his mind and body were dedicated to the safety of the ship and the execution of his orders. He must weld those individuals into a smooth-working machine, able to obey and execute his orders unquestioningly. That was the captain's side of the bargain.

The men looked at Cook.

> Plain and unassuming in his manners and appearance. His stature was upwards of six foot, and his general aspect good looking. His head was small; he wore his hair, which was brown, tied behind; his face was full of expression, his nose exceedingly well-shaped; his eyes, which were small and of a brown colour, were quick and piercing; his eyebrows prominent, which gave his countenance altogether an air of austerity.

For better or for worse, their Captain.

Everything was now set for the little Whitby collier to sail forth on the greatest voyage of exploration and science ever organized by Britain, and Cook received his sailing orders.

Meanwhile Wallis had returned from the Pacific and on his suggestion the newly discovered island of Tahiti was adopted as the most suitable spot for the observations. Cook's orders were interesting and divided into two parts. The first part was public property, prepared by the "Commissioners for executing the Office of the Lord High Admiral" in conjunction with the Royal Society. Lieutenant James Cook was ordered to sail to Tahiti by the Cape Horn route and given permission to revictual at certain places on the way out. He was to receive on board "such persons as the Royal Society should think fit to appoint to observe the passage of the planet Venus over the disk of the sun." It also specified that he was to reach Tahiti at least a month before the 3rd of June, 1769, the date on which the eclipse was expected, and render every possible assistance to the astronomers to ensure that the best results possible were obtained of the transit. The second part of the instructions were highly secret. "When this service is performed [i.e., the observation], you are to put to sea without loss of time and carry into execution the Additional Instructions contained in the enclosed sealed packet." The secret instructions ordered Cook to sail south, then westward, and find out positively whether Terra Australis existed. "There is reason to believe that a Continent, or land of great extent, may be found to the southwards of the tracts of former navigators." They continue:

> You are to proceed southward in order to make discovery of the continent above mentioned until you arrive in the latitude of 40°; not having discovered it in that run, you are to proceed in search of it to the westward, between the latitude before mentioned and the latitude of 35° until you discover it or fall in with the Eastern side of the land discovered by Tasman and now called New Zealand.

The Admiralty demanded the fullest report of any new land found, the coast charted and surveyed, an exact account of the animals should there be any, the nature of the soil, all minerals to be noted and samples brought home.

> You are likewise to observe the genius, temper, disposition and number of the natives, if there be any, and endeavour by all proper means to cultivate a friendship and

alliance with them, making them presents of such Traffic and showing them every kind of civility and regard; taking care, however, not to suffer yourself to be surprised by them, but to be always upon your guard against any accident. You are also with the consent of the natives to take possession of convenient situations in the country, in the name of the King of Great Britain; or, if you find the country uninhabited, take possession for his Majesty by setting up proper marks and descriptions, as first discoverers and possessors.

The moment had arrived. "On Friday the 26th August, the wind becoming fair, we got under sail and put to sea."

The strong, bluff bows of His Majesty's Ship *Endeavour* steered south, the men faced north and took a last, long look at the shores of England. The ship groaned and creaked as she came to life, riding the waves; above the cobweb of rigging and white tautened sails, the gulls screamed and whirled, until they were left behind and only their cries remained, and that, too, faded.

Then the men faced forward and looked south at the great rolling, endless Atlantic. The break was complete and absolute. That morning the little ship had been a part of England, joined to the old country by good strong ropes. They had only to walk down the gangway and across the quayside to guzzle as much ale as their bellies could hold. Now they were a tiny island of timber, the minutest crumb broken from the loaf. Themselves a little separate country with its own laws and king. Whatever blessings or complications there had been ashore, however delightful the soft-lipped embraces of their sweethearts had been, or the acid naggings of the old women, they were broken now, as surely and quickly as the snapping of a rope.

For Cook, there was the inevitable isolation of being Captain; the limits of familiarity with his officers and men were small. His authority depended on keeping himself aloof and apart from them. There was nothing snobbish about this, it was a well-tried and necessary attitude for the Captain to adopt, just as with royalty. For any Captain to become too friendly with his ship's company would be as odd and injurious to his authority as a high court judge descending from his dais, hobnobbing with the prisoner, then expecting to return to his seat and retain the same dignity.

> On the 31st we saw several of the birds which the sailors call "Mother Carey's Chickens" and which they suppose to be the forerunners of a storm; and on the next day we had a very bad gale which brought us under our courses, washed overboard a small boat belonging to the boatswain, and drowned three or four dozen of our poultry, which we regretted still more.

Lieutenants Hicks and Gore no longer smiled grimly; they watched with satisfaction Mother Carey's Chickens. They were pleased to notice salted pork for dinner and trusted it would be sufficiently fat. It gave them great satisfaction to feel the increasingly erratic motion of the deck under their feet and when they sat down to eat, nothing could be more delightful than to watch the greasy meat slithering naughtily about on the plates. That night as Lieutenants Gore and Hicks made the best of their way to their bunks, they were enchanted by the retching groans and gently splashing plops issuing from the civilians' cabins. Their moment had come.

IV

PASSAGE TO RIO DE JANEIRO

August–December, 1768

As part of her stores *Endeavour* carried every chart, book and scrap of evidence relative to the Pacific, and doubtless the perusal of these papers occupied the officers and gentlemen during their leisure hours. So while she ploughs her way south and the ship's company shake themselves down into the comfortable routine of three watches — four hours on and eight off — we will go aft to the wardroom and take a look at the colourful history of the Pacific.

It is a fantastic story of courage, mixed with fervent religion, chivalry, barbaric cruelty and pathos. Of cranky explorers like Quiros, who refused to give his helmsman a course because he said God would guide them. Of Exquemelin, the surgeon-cum-pirate, who, it is reputed, would tear out a man's heart and chew it, or stand up a row of Spaniards and execute them one at a time, licking the dripping blood from his cutlass between each execution. His friend Roc Brasiliano, who, when sober, was "beloved and respected by all" but when dealing with Spaniards would roast them alive for refusing to tell him where he could revictual his ship; men who solemnly attended Mass in captured ports and then proceeded to rape, pillage, and massacre the inhabitants. In that vast ocean, islands were found and lost for 200 years. No stretch of the imagination was too great. From these seas, Solomon was supposed to have wrested his fortune, for, in 1568, Mendaña discovered a group of islands, believed to contain all the treasures of the earth, and called them the Solomon Isles. And so they remain to this day, mute evidence of the supposed wealth that drew adventurers from all ages and walks of life to risk death and incredible hardships.

Balboa is the first European supposed to have seen the great ocean. In 1513 he crossed the Isthmus of Panama and looked over that vast, endless "South Sea." Then, striking his sword on the water, claimed it for Spain. Seven years later Magellan passed through the straits and named the ocean the Pacific.

There is no real evidence that the Portuguese sailed down the east coast of Australia. If they did they kept quiet about it, probably for security reasons, or perhaps the lands contained none of the riches they hoped for. But maps made by the French about 1530 do show a land in the Pacific, where the coastline corresponds in places with the outline of Australia. Gold and spices were what the Europeans sought. Thorne writes of "lands and islands situated between the tropics and the equinoctial [equator]. The richest lands and island in the world, of gold, precious stones, balms, spices, and other things that we here esteem most." The Elizabethans were "assured to expect gold, silver, pearls, rich grain, and such most precious merchandise besides countries of most excellent temperature to be inhabited."

The Pope, with one sweeping gesture, split the mighty

Pacific in two, gave half to Spain, and half to Portugal, much to the annoyance of Queen Elizabeth, who claimed that all ships, save her own, were trespassing. So out from England came that gallant, courageous succession of sea captains: Frobisher and Drake, the first Englishman to round Cape Horn in the *Golden Hind,* a most appropriate name, for he fitted the little ship out with regal splendour. His cabin was decorated with silver and gold fixtures, and he even took along a small orchestra of "experte musitians" to entertain himself and the ship's company. "All the vessels for his table, yea even belonging to the cooke-roome, being of pure silver and diverse shewes of all sorts of curious workmanship." Moreover, he made it his particular diversion personally to execute any Spaniard who was unfortunate enough to fall into his hands. Thomas Cavendish and Richard Hawkins, the last Englishman to enter the Pacific for many a long year, sent with their Queen's blessing to harry and rob the Spaniards. "My deare Pyrat," Elizabeth addresses Drake.

That brave fool, Torres, driving his tiny ship between New Guinea and Australia from east to west to prove the existence of a passage. He had no hope of turning back if the two countries were joined together, as was commonly believed, for the wind blew always from the east. His secret lay hidden for nearly 200 years until Dalrymple unearthed it and Cook proved it. Diego de Prado, a Spanish officer who accompanied Torres, confirmed the discovery (but the confirmation only came to light in 1930).

The Dutchman, Janszoon, probably sailed down a part of eastern Australia and called the land New Holland. Tasman discovered the island named after him, then went on to

Staaten Land, or New Zealand; he apparently decided that Australia and New Guinea were all one continent. After Janszoon the Pacific faded in importance to the European countries. They had plenty on their plates, founding colonies in the Americas and East Indies. It is not until 1699 that any real interest was again taken in the Pacific, when the Admiralty sent out its first scientific expedition, under the weak-willed civilian Dampier. He had already published a book on the Pacific which proved extremely popular (the first in English since Sir Richard Hawkins' *Observations* in 1594). But his voyage achieved little, the ship left England half rotten, totally unfitted for a long cruise; the crew were bad and had no heart for the adventure and Dampier, commanding a ship for the first time, was a failure. He was much more successful as a writer and on his return published a second book, *Voyages and Discovery*. A little later he produced two further volumes, *Voyages to New Holland*. Books that were widely and eagerly read, they could be termed best-sellers, for educated Europe was suffering from a form of cultural indigestion; they dreamed of the undiscovered lands as an earthly Paradise, peopled by the "noble savage," free from the intrigues and vices of their own royal courts. De Brosse, a French writer, got himself so enraptured with the pure, innocent way of life he imagined existed in the southern continent that he wrote a book seriously advocating that criminals should be sent there, for he believed, with all sincerity, that their evil ways would fall from them merely by imbibing for a year or two the pure, guiltless atmosphere of the new lands. They could then return to Europe, reformed and worthy citizens. Terra Australis was another enchanted world; the most fantastic tales were invented and accepted as fact. As with interplanetary travel today, the bigger the lie the more likely it was to be swallowed.

The war of the Spanish Succession put an end to exploration in the Pacific, and England turned her attention to the more lucrative pastime of robbing the Spaniard. The great Manila galleons of Spain were glittering prizes, treasure ships carrying cargoes of gold, silver, and precious stones valued at tens of thousands of pounds, and ships of the Royal Navy entering the Pacific at this time were thinly disguised pirates. Commodore Anson and Captain Woodes Roger took their share of Spanish wealth and, luckily for Cook, captured quite a few charts and maps. In return, the relentless South Seas exacted a dreadful toll of death, for rarely did a vessel reach England without losing at least fifty per cent of her crew.

With the end of the Seven Years' War Europe again turned her attention to the problems of the Pacific and the finding of the mythical Northwest Passage. From England came Byron, but apart from discovering a few islands, his voyage added little to what was already known. The Russians sent Bering, and the Dutch had one last fling in the person of Captain Jacob Roggeveen, the discoverer of Easter Island, a curious dot of land containing odd stone statues of unknown origin. (The mystery of those statues was left unsolved until the twentieth century, when Thor Heyerdahl and his gallant comrades bounced across thousands of miles of the Pacific on their tiny raft, *Kon-Tiki,* and gave us a reasonable and convincing answer to their origin.)

The Pacific expedition immediately preceding Cook's

voyage was commanded by Captains Wallis and Carteret, each equipped with a ship as rotten as a dunghill. It is to the credit of these two seamen and the shame of the Admiralty that they managed to take their mouldering vessels round the world. Unfortunately they lost each other in the Magellan Straits. Wallis discovered the paradise of Tahiti. He and his men enjoyed to the full the fresh food of the island and the willing favours of the Tahitan maidens. In return they left behind disease. Captain Carteret was less fortunate, his course took him far to the south of Tahiti, and he continued to search in those waters until the scurvy and sickness of his ship's company, together with the appalling condition of his leaky vessel, inappropriately named the *Swallow,* forced him north to Batavia for repairs and recuperation. The dockyard authorities there told him it was madness to attempt to sail his rotten ship home, but that was not the way of the Royal Navy and he managed to get her safely back to England nearly a year later than Wallis, and after Cook had sailed. It had been a hard, exacting voyage; his only important discovery was rather negative. He had sailed through a portion of the Pacific never before navigated and carved off a large lump of ocean where the elusive southern continent was not. In addition, he had rediscovered the Solomons after a lapse of 200 years.

There is just one more explorer of note who deserves mention, although his discoveries were not available to Cook either — the French aristocrat Bougainville, sometime lawyer, diplomat, and soldier, in which capacity he had opposed Cook at the storming of Quebec. He was not a professional sailor, but came nearer than most to unravelling the secrets of the Pacific. The final solution was left to the English farm labourer's son who outclassed the nobility of France. Bougainville was at sea at the same time as both Wallis and Carteret, and Cook, too. He followed closely on the tracks of Wallis as far as Tahiti, arriving there about a year after him. The natives told him of their previous visitor, indulged the carnal lusts of his sailors and received the customary European payment of venereal disease. Thereafter Bougainville followed the trail of Carteret and eventually overhauled him in the Atlantic. The two ships exchanged polite salutations, but said nothing about their respective voyages. Bougainville, of course, knew all about Carteret's travels and the English captain was able to learn all he wanted to know from the over-garrulous chatter of a French boat's crew.

Meanwhile *Endeavour* continued to plough her way south. Each day the men could detect the increasing heat of the sun and their bodies became brown and hard, toughened by sun, sea, and work. Aft, in the wardroom, the officers and gentlemen scratched their heads in bewilderment at the conflicting mass of evidence they had read, for there had been no attempt at any sort of international exchange of ideas or information; on the contrary, European nations were reticent about discoveries they made. The charting of newfound lands was bad and inaccurate, islands were placed hundreds of miles from their correct positions and frequently not recognized when rediscovered. The majority of eminent geographers were armchair gentlemen who would dismiss with a stroke of their pens any new discoveries that did not fit in with their own pet theories. To complicate matters still further for Cook, some nations deliberately put about false information to confuse their neighbors. Tahiti was the only positive evidence *Endeavour's* captain could rely on; thereafter he was alone, but those were difficulties to be dealt with as they arose. For the moment the main task was to get the ship safely to Madeira, the first port of call. Here it was hoped to revictual and take aboard an ample stock of the good Madeira wine, which for many years had been found to keep at sea better than others.

On the 12th of September they sighted the beautiful vineclad hills of Madeira, rising almost as high as the eye could see, bathed in a sunlight that turned the green of the vineyards into every shade of colour, down to the deep purple depths of the valleys. It looked as fresh and lovely as the shore always does from seaward, after even a fortnight on the water. But the first serious accident awaited them. On anchoring, Mr. Wier, the Master's Mate, was carried overboard by the buoy rope and went to bottom with the anchor. The seamen hurled themselves at the capstan and pushed until their lungs burst against the stubborn weight of the cable; they were too late, the body came up entangled in the buoy rope, but it was dead.

It has never been the way of the sea to mourn overlong. The tragedy had been quick and final and was soon forgotten, and the ship's company made the most of their run ashore, seeing the sights, eating and drinking. Cook describes a chapel he was shown in a convent, the walls and ceiling of which were entirely lined with human skulls and thighbones; the thighbones were laid across each other and a skull placed in each of the four angles. One skull in particular interested him, for it appeared that the upper and lower jaws were joined together so firmly that to feed the man it had been necessary to knock out the teeth on one side of the face, a clumsy operation that had also injured the jaw.

The work of storing ship continued and on the 18th of September *Endeavour* again headed out to sea and set course for South America, her belly comfortably filled with a supply of fresh fruit, water, 270 pounds of fresh meat, a live bullock, and ten tons of wine.

They were always steering south, until the men aboard began to feel that this existence had forever been their sphere, like a small village wholly dependent on itself and crafts to keep alive. A walk of a few yards forward to the carpenter's shop took the place of a stroll down the village street, and instead of pausing on the way home to look at a neighbour's pigs they rested their elbows on the taffrail and watched the sea bubble and chuckle along the ship's side. Everything was shortened; within weeks the crew knew each other as well as if they had lived a lifetime together. The seasons shrank to four hours on watch and eight hours off, and a scramble aloft to the crow's nest gave them an isolation as complete as that of a man on the top of a mountain. On calm days off duty, they yarned and smoked with a messmate for half an hour on the port side, then strolled thirty feet to the starboard side; the sea looked just the same, but it had been quite a walk, in fact the whole breadth of their tiny country.

The same feeling crept into the wardroom, for each evening on the little ship the delicious ceremony of dinner assumed the importance of a long awaited banquet. It was the turning point of the day when conversation and laughter rumbled round the table or drifted drowsily into reminiscences of home as the Madeira livened and softened their moods. At this hour, the Captain could come as near to familiarity as he dared, half listening to the talk, and half subconsciously ever alert to the swing of the lantern on the deckhead. Perhaps a last fragrant pipeful and a stroll round the upper deck before turning in if the elements were kind, or, at any moment, the cry of "Captain, sir, storm ahead!" For in tropical waters the fury of the winds might beat up to a mad tempest in minutes, sending every man flying to his station aloft to shorten sail and fight with wildly lashing canvas that could fling them unnoticed into the sea; hanging on to halyards with tooth and nail till the live ropes burned the skin off their hands; working by the vivid stabs of forked lightning capable of tearing the sails to shreds, or if the seams held against the power of the storm, bringing the masts crashing down on the decks in a horrible confusion of canvas, ropes, and men, leaving them at the mercy of the storm. At such moments the officers and sailors united against a common enemy with one object: get in sail.

Fortunately for *Endeavour* the weather remained kind on this leg of the voyage. It was now nearly three weeks since they had left Madeira and Cook determined to call at Rio de Janeiro to top up his stores and fresh water before rounding Cape Horn. On the 12th of October the ship nosed her way into the Bay of Rio de Janeiro, and at nine o'clock in the morning Cook sent ashore his First Lieutenant, Mr. Hicks, with a note to the Portuguese governor listing their requirements and also asking permission for the scientists aboard to land and collect botanical specimens. By midday the pinnace had not returned, and as the hot afternoon wore on, still with no sign of the return of Mr. Hicks, Cook became a little worried. At five in the evening the pinnace was sighted, and the Captain cursed himself for worrying over such a triviality, but as the boat drew alongside it became evident that the First Lieutenant was not there; instead, a Portuguese officer stepped aboard. The pinnace was closely followed by a ten-oared boat full of armed soldiers which immediately proceeded to circle slowly round the ship. Cook's uneasiness grew and the Portuguese officer did little to relieve the tension when he informed the Captain that his Lieutenant was being held ashore pending a full statement of their business and destination. If the facts satisfied the Governor then Mr. Hicks would be released next day and the business of storing ship started. Cook was left with no option but to comply with the Governor's demand, and he gave an honest account of their intentions. The crew were angry and disappointed with the unwelcome news and the refusal to allow them ashore after so many days at sea, and the wardroom buzzed with indignation at their uncourteous reception. For the time being nothing could be done; they were a small ship, lightly armed, and well within range of the shore batteries. To up anchor and run for it was unthinkable. Even if they were not blasted to pieces the First Lieutenant was held prisoner ashore and any attempt to rescue him would be doomed before it started. All the time the sinister shape of the guardboat crept stealthily round them, the moon glinting on the weapons of the soldiers. The situation was tricky and must be handled carefully. Cook realized that a mistake on his part might end in disaster before they even reached the Pacific. At home *Endeavour* would not be missed for at least two years.

The next morning Captain Cook went ashore and had a personal interview with the Governor, who continued to be unhelpful. Mr. Hicks was released but Cook got the impression that His Excellency did not believe his story and suspected them of illegal trading. He refused point-blank to allow anyone ashore from the ship, except the seamen actually engaged on re-victualling and they were to be accompanied by a Portuguese guard. Furthermore, all stores must be bought through the Governor. Disappointed, Cook left the palace; a disappointment that turned to resentment when he realized he was being followed everywhere by an officer.

> As soon as I took leave of His Excellency I found an officer who had orders to follow me wherever I went; of this I desired an explanation and was told that it was meant as a compliment. I earnestly desired to be excused from accepting such an honour, but the good viceroy would by no means suffer it to be disposed with.

Cook deserves full marks for keeping his temper.

A further exchange of letters did nothing to ease the situation. Cook's suspicions that the Governor did not believe his story was confirmed with a final slap in the face to the British, for the Viceroy "expressed some doubts whether the *Endeavour,* considering her structure and other circumstances, was in the service of His Majesty." This was a little too much on top of the insults they had already received, Mr. Banks and his friends were prevented from leaving the ship; there was the galling presence of a Portuguese officer who always accompanied the pinnace, and in addition that confounded boat, loaded with armed soldiers, continually circling the ship. "Right," thought Cook, "we will try his Excellency's bluff." So he gave orders that his First Lieutenant was to resist forcibly the presence of the foreign officers in the boat. The result was disastrous and ended by *Endeavour* having her pinnace and crew impounded and Mr. Hicks ingloriously sent back in another boat.

Now the British are notably a stubborn race and the irrepressible Banks was no exception to the rule. Whatever the risks, get ashore he would, and did. Aided and abetted by the Captain and a boat's crew he somehow managed to evade the watchful eyes of the armed guardboat, sneak stealthily shoreward and land unnoticed. Like an overgrown schoolboy, Banks bought a fat hog for eleven shillings as a reward to the sailors, and a Muscovy duck to relieve the monotony of the menu in the wardroom. The whole delicate operation was successfully concluded by again dodging the guard boat and getting the booty aboard without incident. The blessed porker must have had the added deliciousness of a salmon poached out of season, or an apple stolen from the vicar's garden on a Sunday. The seamen roared with delight and laughed till their sides ached as they stuffed themselves with fresh fat pork and the good, warm grease trickled over their chins. Aft in the wardroom, no doubt, the roast duck went down equally well, as did the stock of Madeira; the officers shouted their approval and drank the health of His Majesty, the brave Banks, and the damnation of the arrogant Portuguese.

To date, historians seem to have overlooked this daring invasion of South America by the British, and though it is probably not the most important, it should go on record as quite the sauciest.

From a remark Cook wrote it would appear that fat pork and Muscovy duck were not the only delight Banks and Solander met ashore.

> It is I believe, universally allowed that the women, both of Spanish and Portuguese settlements in South America, make less difficulty of granting personal favours than those of any other civilized country in the world. Of the ladies of this town some have formed so unfavourable opinion as to declare that they did not believe there was a modest one amongst them. This censure is certainly too general, but what Dr. Solander saw of them when he was ashore gave him no very excellent idea of their chastity; he told me that as soon as it was dark one or more of them appeared in every window and distinguished those whom they liked among the gentlemen that walked past them by giving them nosegays; that he and two gentlemen who were with him, received so many of these favours that, at the end of their walk, which was not a long one, they threw whole hatfuls away. Great allowance must certainly be made for local customs, that which, in one country, would be an indecent familiarity is a mere act of general courtesy in another; of the fact, therefore, which

I have related, I shall say nothing but that I am confident it is true.

As the days passed and *Endeavour's* stay at Rio lengthened into weeks, Cook and his men had the chance to observe the customs and livelihood of the Portuguese; neither seems to have much impressed Cook. Ashore, murder among the population appeared a common crime, and as long as the criminal could get safely to the sanctuary of a church, he was safe. The coxswain told a story typical of the hot-blooded Latins. "One day looking at two men who appeared to be talking together in a friendly manner, I saw that one of them suddenly drew a knife, and stabbed the other, who, not instantly falling, was attacked again by the murderer who withdrew the knife and stabbed him a second time."

Even the local farms and cattle came in for criticism, and Cook, judging them with the practised eye of a farmer, wrote: "Most of the land, as far as we saw of the country, is laid down in grass, upon which cattle are pastured in great plenty; but they are so lean that an Englishman will scarcely eat of their flesh."

The reasons, too, for the Viceroy's extreme caution in allowing them ashore became apparent. The country inland was rich in gold and precious stones; His Excellency went to great lengths to ensure that the treasures passed through no one's hand but his own. Only a certain amount was allowed to be dug each year, but at a dreadful price in human flesh and suffering, for no less than 40,000 Negroes were annually imported on the King's account, and on one occasion, owing to a devastating outbreak of disease, their number had to be supplemented by a further 20,000 from Rio. The figures were all the more horrible when the crew learned that it generally took only about a month to mine the allowed amount of gold and stones. After that, anyone found in the precious districts, on any pretense, before the next year, was immediately put to death. As a further insurance against unauthorized persons penetrating inland the regular officers kept the civilians in place, and in turn the Governor effectively restricted the movements of the soldiers.

> To the regulars the inhabitants behave with the utmost humility and submission; and I was told that if any man should neglect to take off his hat upon meeting an officer, he would immediately be knocked down — but the subordination of the officers themselves to the Viceroy is enforced with circumstances equally mortifying, for they are obliged to attend in his hall three times every day to ask his commands; the answer constantly is "There is nothing new," and I have been told that this servile attendance is exacted to prevent their going into the country; and, if so, it effectually answers the purpose.

For three weeks *Endeavour* had lain frustrated and impatient in the harbour of Rio, but now at last she was ready to sail. Nothing could have been more irritating than to have been anchored a few hundred yards off shore with the men unable to stretch their legs; far better to be at sea. Cook had acted with admirable patience and tact and was heartily glad to request a pilot and tow down the river. The 5th of December was a breathlessly calm day, the air loaded with butterflies, and a general feeling of release and expectancy livened the crew. As the ship neared the last fort the men made ready to hoist sail and stand out to sea; they knew little and cared less of what lay ahead of them but it would have to be bad if it were to surpass the boredom they had suffered during the last three weeks.

Then, from the fort, to the utter amazement of all aboard, a cannon thundered out sending a plume of water ahead of their bows. *Endeavour* hove to, only to find that poor liaison, or a complete lack of it, between the Viceroy and the fort prevented their sailing. The fort commander would not let them pass without the Governor's permission, which he had not received. For two days they sweated and fumed while the Portuguese authorities dawdled through their tortuous system, but finally the sailing orders arrived, the pilot left them, and at the same moment the guard boat, which had hovered about them from the first hour of their arrival to the last, slipped astern and out of sight. With the stoical phlegm of the North Country, Cook watched the hated galley fade from view, then lowered his own boat and sent Mr. Banks inshore to collect butterflies and plants to his heart's content. Another hour or two of delay would make little difference and Cook was hanged if he was going to be kept loitering for three weeks only to run the moment he was ordered. When the boat returned she was hoisted aboard and *Endeavour* stood out to sea.

V

ROUNDING CAPE HORN

January–March, 1769

ENDEAVOUR continued her southerly course with little to break the monotony of routine watch-keeping except the great numbers of penguins, albatross, and sheerwaters, seals, whales and porpoises they saw, and the odd shark or two they caught from the stern. The gentlemen engaged themselves with taking specimens from the sea and examining them under the microscope. Cook kept the ship's company busy bending a new set of sails, for they were steering towards Tierra del Fuego and expected dirty weather rounding the dreaded Cape Horn. They judged themselves to be now opposite the "Baye sans fond" where the fertile brain of Mr. Dalrymple "supposes there is a passage quite through the continent of America." Needless to say, as with most of his theories, he was mistaken.

The weather was becoming appreciably chillier and "the people now beginning to complain of cold, each of them received what is called a Magellanic jacket and a pair of trousers. The jacket is made of a thick woollen stuff called 'Fearnought.'" Cook was taking no chances with the health of his crew.

On the 11th they sighted the mountains of Tierra del Fuego, after nearly a month at sea, and on the 14th Cook attempted to enter the strait of Le Maire, but terrific, pounding waves and a strong current drove them back out to sea. The fury of the storm built up the breakers so that they "had exactly the appearance as they would have had if they had broke over a ledge of rocks; and when the ship was in this torrent she frequently pitched so that the bowsprit was under the water."

Remembering his instructions to help the scientific staff whenever possible, Cook tried to find an anchorage, but without success; finally he sent Banks and Dr. Solander ashore in a boat to collect specimens and in an afternoon the two botanists obtained a hundred samples of plants never before known to Europeans.

After searching another day and trying several spots, *Endeavour* eventually anchored in the Bay of Good Success. Cook, Banks, Solander, and a party of seamen landed after dinner, ostensibly to look for fresh water, but also in an attempt to trade with the Indians, for there was quite a crowd of them on the beach; they ran, however, at the approach of the English, and Banks determined to try his hand, for the first time, at dealing with the savages. He had no idea what to expect, but trusting to luck he and Solander slowly advanced a couple of hundred yards ahead of the party; it took considerable courage, for neither of them knew if the inhabitants had ever seen white people before or what their reactions might be. The notion worked; in a couple of minutes two Indians came towards them, stopped a short distance away, squatted on their haunches, then threw behind them a few sticks they carried. The English took this as a sign that they had abandoned their weapons and the assumption proved correct, because the natives walked briskly away, beckoning the gentlemen to follow. This they did and were "received with many uncouth signs of friendship." In return Banks gave them beads and ribbon, which seemed to delight them. "A mutual confidence and good will being thus produced, our parties joined; the conversation, such as it was, became general." Despite the fact that neither side understood a word of the other's language, the natives made up for the lack of a common tongue by shouting with all the force of their lungs, but without directing their voices either at the English or their companions. They impressed Cook as about the dullest collection of brainless humans he had met, for nothing they were shown interested or amazed them and they seemed to possess an intelligence little above animals'; any sign of curiosity was entirely lacking in their mental make-up. The Captain supposed their vacant indifference to be due to the drabness of the country and the inhospitability of the climate.

The next day it was decided to make an expedition as far inland as they could march in a day. The country appeared to be well wooded near the coast, followed by a strip of open pastureland, dwindling into the barren rock of the hilltops. Banks hoped that those rocks would yield an abundant supply of unknown alpine plants.

The party consisted of Banks, Dr. Solander, with attendants and servants, two seamen to assist in carrying the baggage, Mr. Monkhouse, the surgeon, and Mr. Green, the astronomer. They set off early in the morning, climbing up through the woods in clear, sunny weather. The first snag arose when they came to the supposed pastureland, which turned out to be a bog covered with short stumpy bushes about three feet high, so tough and stubborn that it was impossible to push through them. The only way to cross the swamp was to lift their legs over the bushes, which would not yield an inch, then sink knee-deep in the black, oozy mud and gather enough strength to draw their feet out of the sucking slime for the next step forward. Banks, of course, was not in the least deterred by the conditions and urged the party forward, confident that the next few steps would bring them to easier conditions. But the firm rocky summit seemed to get no nearer and they were tiring. To make matters worse the weather, which had been like a fine May day, deteriorated into a gloomy coldness with sudden blasts of icy, piercing wind, laden with stinging, driven snow. Still they pushed on, certain now that they were three quarters of the way across. Suddenly Buchan, one of the draughtsmen, fell writhing in the mud, seized with a slobbering fit. There was nothing for it but to stop. Banks should have seen the red light, for the weather was worsening and most of the party were achingly fatigued by dragging their limbs and loads through the cloying slush. Instead of returning to the ship, he decided to light a fire for Buchan and leave behind the tiredest members of the party to look after him. Meanwhile, he, Solander, Green and the surgeon would press on to the summit and gather the specimens.

Their efforts were well rewarded. They found themselves in a veritable botanist's paradise crammed with a magnificent selection of alpine plants totally unknown to Europe. They were seized with an almost drunken desire to gather a sample of every plant on the hilltop and worked with an intensity regardless of time, the increasing cold or the added frequency of the snow-laden blasts. At last, straightening their backs, they realized with horror that it would be quite impossible to regain the ship that night. Yet even now Banks could not call it a day, and despite the fact that the cold had increased to a numbing intensity he sent Green and Monkhouse to see how Buchan was faring, while he and Solander continued to gather plants. It was a foolish decision, only excusable by his youth and a burning enthusiasm for the job.

From their vantage point they could see a small hill that looked a better place from which to cross the swamp. They arranged to meet there, wade through the marsh to the woods, light a fire, and spend the night in the shelter of the forest. The plan was reasonable enough, for the swamp looked barely half a mile wide, and since this time the going was downhill they did not anticipate any great difficulties.

By eight o'clock they were all gathered at the rendezvous and, though pinched with cold, seemed happy and strong enough, including Buchan, to make the crossing. Luckily Dr. Solander was an experienced mountaineer and had several times crossed the mountains between Norway and Sweden. He knew only too well the effects of extreme cold coupled with fatigue. A dreadful numbness that crept over the mind and body, building up to an irresistible desire to lie down and sleep, even to die, for the brain froze into a languid torpor that refused to give orders. He warned them that however painful it might be they must keep moving, and to resist at all costs the feeling that a few minutes' rest would revive them. "Whoever sits down," says he, "will sleep; and whoever sleeps will wake no more."

Admonished and alarmed they set forward, but even before they reached the swamp and within minutes of the strong warning Solander had given them, he himself was overcome by the dreadful symptoms. He lay down in the snow and declared himself unable to go farther. Banks, bringing up the rear, found him, but nothing he could do would get him on his feet and it was only with the greatest difficulty, at first by pleading, then swearing and punching, that he managed to keep Solander awake. Richmond, one of the black servants, came next and sank to the ground in a coma. Half frantic with worry Banks sent the party forward to light a fire and stayed behind with four others to look after Solander and Richmond. Somehow they managed to kick and drag the men to their feet, now as helpless as toddling infants and as stubborn and unreasoning as petulant children. It took a tremendous effort to drag their own leaden limbs through the grasping mire, but to keep the two cold-drunken, bitterly protesting men moving, sapped the very life from their overtired bodies. Round them the storm increased in a mad crescendo of icy fury as if determined to kill and devour its victims then and there. Finally all efforts failed; Solander and Richmond slipped to the ground, their will-power gone. Despite frantic threats that to remain was death the Negro servant declared he longed to die, and Solander, despite his warning, mumbled the impossibility of his continuing without rest. Within a minute both were in a profound sleep. Desperately the men worked to revive them, fighting with insensible lumps of humanity drifting quickly through oblivion to death. With mad strength they tried to lift and carry them, but it was hopeless, the weight of the bodies burst their lungs and spread-eagled them face downward in the stinking black mud.

After a period that stretched into eternity, but was in fact only a few minutes, the main party returned with the welcome news that they had got a fire going a quarter of a mile away. A last, despairing effort to wake Richmond failed, but miraculously Solander regained consciousness, and though he had only slept for five minutes his limbs and muscles were so shrunk with cold that his boots fell from his feet. Reluctantly Banks left Richmond to the care of the other Negro servant and a sailor who had suffered less from the cold. Promising to send help as soon as they got to the fire, the whole party set off half dragging, half carrying the crippled Solander over the last stumbling quarter-mile of swamp. They got him to the fire and sent two seamen back for Richmond, but in half an hour they returned, for despite continual shouting they had been unable to find them and since Banks had not been able to trace a bottle of rum which he wanted to serve out, he concluded that the alcohol was in the pack of one of the missing men; they had probably over indulged themselves and wandered off in a vain attempt to find the fire.

A further two hours' heavy fall of snow convinced them that any hope of the missing men's surviving was gone, but at midnight Banks believed he heard a faint cry and excitably, unbelieving, hushed the party. There it was again, and this time there was no mistaking the muffled shout for help. Immediately Banks and four others fought their way towards the voice; to their great joy they found the seaman with just sufficient strength left to put one foot in front of the other and cry for help. Banks sent him back to the fire and guided by his direction made off to look for the two Negroes, with instructions to send on as many men as possible. They found them still alive, one lying down and the other standing up, but quite unable to move a muscle; they were both rigid and insensible as stone. The combined efforts of the party failed to move them, for the snow was now waist-deep and still falling, the night utterly black and the unseen stunted bushes proved an obstacle beyond their strength. They tried to light a fire, tried to carry some of the main fire to them, but the falling snow won.

They had been away for one and a half hours, and the bitter cold was producing its awful symptoms again. Several of the party began to lose their sensibility, and one Briscoe was so ill that they thought he must die before they could get him to the fire. As a last hopeless resort they made a bed of boughs for the two Negroes, covering them with more branches, and left them to certain death.

Back at the fire Banks slumped down and burying his head in his hand, cursed himself for his own stupid folly which had brought them to this dreadful plight. If only he had turned back when Buchan fell with a fit. Why, oh why, had he gone on gathering plants while the weather worsened around them? If only he and Solander had not delayed that extra hour after he sent back Green and Monkhouse. No use to ask himself now; it was too late and worse might lie before them.

The account Cook wrote down as given to him by Banks, of the miseries of that endless, bitter night tells most poignantly the dreadful doubts that assailed him, for they

> passed the night in a situation, which, however dreadful in itself, was rendered more afflicting by the remembrance

of what was past, and the uncertainty of what was to come. Of twelve, the number that set out together in health and spirits, two were supposed to be already dead; a third was so ill that it was doubtful whether he would be able to go forward in the morning; and a fourth, Mr. Buchan, was in danger of a return of his fits by fresh fatigue after so uncomfortable a night; they were distant from the ship a long day's journey through pathless woods in which it was too probable they might be bewildered till they were overtaken by the next night; and, not having prepared for a journey of more than eight or ten hours, they were wholly destitute of provisions, except a vulture, which they happened to shoot while they were out and which, if equally divided, would not afford each of them half a meal; and they knew not how much more they might suffer from cold, as snow still continued to fall.

When the morning dawned, they saw nothing round them, as far as the eye could reach, but snow, which seemed to lie as thick upon the trees as upon the ground; and the blasts returned so frequently and with such violence, that they found it impossible for them to set out: how long this might last they knew not, and they had but too much reason to apprehend that it would confine them in that desolate forest till they perished with hunger and cold.

At six o'clock that morning they thought they detected a faint glimmer of sunshine through the clouds and Banks despatched two men to find out if the Negroes had survived; but they were dead. Snow was still falling and a start impossible; Briscoe remained very ill, though protesting that he thought he could make it if conditions improved; Buchan was in far better spirits than they dared to hope. By about eight o'clock a small regular breeze sprang up and the sun was definitely stronger. They noticed with heartfelt relief the air clearing and large chunks of snow slipping from the trees, a certain sign that a thaw was approaching.

Hunger was the pressing problem and they decided that they must eat before attempting the march to the ship, so the vulture was split up into equal portions and each man given his share, raw, to cook as he pleased. It afforded them scant comfort, and only amounted to three mouthfuls apiece.

They started the journey back at ten o'clock and wept with gratitude when the beach was reached in only three hours. Not till then did they realize that what they had done was to walk right round the mountain, instead of in a straight line up to it. They were soon safely aboard *Endeavour* and "congratulated each other upon their safety with a joy that no man can feel who has not been exposed to equal danger; and as I had suffered great anxiety at their not returning in the evening of the day on which they set out, I was not wholly without my share."

There was little to detain them longer in the bay, and the work of embarking fresh water and food went forward. Banks and Solander continued to collect plants but with more regard to their safety. They visited a native village and walked among the inhabitants with impunity, which was really all wrong, for the experts in London had warned them to expect meetings with a "frightful Colossus" eight feet high, or "enormous goblins" which Captain Byron was supposed to have seen in this place. True, they reported the natives to be large "but clumsily built." Nor was beauty one of their attributes, and Cook surpassed himself in describing their complexions. "Their colour resembles that of rust of iron mixed with dirty oil." But of giants they saw none.

They realized from bits of glass and other odd trinkets found among the Indians that they had had previous exchanges with Europeans, and during dinner one evening, Cook recalled a story about M. Bougainville's visits to the coast, just a year before *Endeavour* arrived. The Frenchman "had, amongst other things, given glass to the people whom he found here; for he says that a boy about twelve years old took it into his head to eat some of it. By this unhappy incident he died in great misery." A slow smile spread over Cook's face and his brown eyes twinkled. . . . "but the endeavours of the good Father, the French Aumonier, were more successful than those of the surgeon, for though the surgeon could not save his life, the charitable priest found means to steal a Christian baptism upon him so secretly that none of his pagan relations knew anything of the matter."

The wardroom roared its approval. That was the best of this Captain, he sat so quietly at table that they never knew what was behind the kindly, handsome face. He might listen silently to them for an hour, arguing some difficult point, then settle their discussions with a few words of profound logic that left them amazed at the brilliance of his mind, or cap their stories with a subtle remark which burst their sides with laughter and kept them chuckling for hours after, for his humour was never unkind, never sarcastic.

They made up the monotony of their diet by the variety of their wit and an open-mindedness in trying out new dishes. From a type of wild celery found on the shores of Tierra del Fuego they seasoned their soup. "It may, indeed, easily be known by the taste, which is between that of celery and parsley. We used the celery in large quantities, particularly in our soup, which, thus medicated, produced the same effect which seamen generally derive from a vegetable diet, after having been long confined to salt provisions."

Banks shot some albatross, "skinned, and having soaked them in salt water till the morning, we parboiled them, then throwing away the liquor, stewed them in a very little fresh water till they were tender, and had them served up with savoury sauce: thus dressed, the dish was universally commended, and we eat of it very heartily, even when there was fresh pork upon the table." Once they found a large cuttlefish, which had just been killed by birds, floating in a mangled condition in the water. "Of this cuttlefish we made one of the best soups we had ever tasted."

By two o'clock on Sunday afternoon of January 22, Cook considered the conditions right to attempt the Strait of Le Maire, for, from the experience of previous seamen, this was likely to prove the most difficult and hazardous part of the voyage. The Captain carefully checked the reports of men who had been through, weighing in his mind the soundness of their advice. He considered Commodore Anson's account. Anson had been overjoyed by a strong flood tide which swept him through the twenty-one-mile strait in two hours, only to be carried back with equal speed by a fierce squall and the turn of the tide. Then for three months he had battled against storm followed by storm to regain that twenty-one miles. Tempests raged with incredible violence, ripping the sails to ribbons and keeping the men in a state of terror, many of whom were killed and wounded by the erratic plunging of the helpless ship. Cook wondered if there was anything to be learned from that? Indeed there was, and he decided it was essential to start the passage the moment the flood tide turned, in the hope that *Endeavour* would be carried through and well clear of the opening into the Pacific before the tide turned and carried her back, as it had done Anson. Of the advice other captains offered, Cook took not the slightest notice and rejected the lot without reservation. He waited till the weather was good and seemed likely to remain so, raising the anchor immediately his ship started to swing round her cable, indicating the turn of the tide, and purposely hugged the coast of Tierra del Fuego throughout the passage, so that he could run for shelter and anchor in the event of the weather worsening. *Endeavour* got through safely, not by chance or coincidence, but by an act of brilliant seamanship, coupled with the fact that her Captain had the courage to carry out his own convictions.

Typically, it was not sufficient for Cook merely to get his own ship safely through, and during the passage he and Mr. Green, the astronomer, made careful observation. Modestly he wrote: "I will, however, venture to assert, that the longitude of few parts of the world is better ascertained than that of the Strait of Le Maire and Cape Horn, in the chart now offered to the public, as it was laid down by several observations of the sun and moon that were made both by myself and Mr. Green."

Soon they felt the gentle up and down movement of the ship, and the soft slop, slop of the swell sliding by the bulge of the bows which meant they had reached the open sea again. The ship was following a general northwesterly track, heading for Tahiti and the all-important observation of Venus. "We now began to have strong gales and heavy seas, with irregular intervals of calm and fine weather." Deceptive spells of clear skies and flat seas that lulled them into a feeling of security and on the lower deck the same tranquillity hid a storm of human emotion, which, from a small, trivial beginning welled into a tragedy.

It is inevitable that when men, for the most part illiterate, without the distraction of books, are cooped together in a small space for long periods, with little to break the monotony of the endless, rolling ocean and routine of watch-keeping, little things assume vast importance. A friendly discussion develops into an argument, a fight. Like children, men under those conditions can be callously cruel, driving a misfit into a hopeless loneliness, and nothing is so soul-destroying as to be lonely in a crowd. But that is the tragic story of a young marine aboard *Endeavour*. The incident greatly distressed Cook, who always treated his crew with decency and a firm kindness.

> On the 25th, about noon, one of the marines, a young fellow about twenty, was placed as sentry at the cabin-door; while he was upon this duty one of my servants was at the same place preparing to cut a piece of seal-skin into tobacco pouches; he had promised one to several of the men, but had refused one to this young fellow, though he had asked him several times; upon which he jocularly

threatened to steal one, if it should be in his power. It happened that the servant being called hastily away gave the skin in charge to the sentinel, without regarding what had passed between them. The sentinel immediately secured a piece of the skin, which the other missing at his return grew angry; but after some altercation, contented himself with taking it away, declaring that, for so trifling an affair, he would not complain of him to the Officers. But it happened that one of his fellow-soldiers, overhearing the dispute, came to the knowledge of what had happened, and told it to the rest, who, taking it into their heads to stand up for the honour of their corps, reproached the offender with great bitterness, and reviled him in the most opprobrious terms; they exaggerated his offence into a crime of the deepest die; they said it was a theft by a sentry when he was upon duty, and of a thing that had been committed to his trust; they declared it a disgrace to associate with him, and the sergeant in particular, said that, if the person from whom the skin had been stolen would not complain, he would complain himself, for that his honour would suffer if the offender was not punished. From the scoffs and reproaches of these men of honour, the poor young fellow retired to his hammock in an agony of confusion and shame. The sergeant soon after went to him and ordered him to follow him to the deck: he obeyed without reply, but, it being in the dusk of the evening, he slipped from the sergeant and went forward: he was seen by some of the people who thought he was gone to the head; (seamen relieved the calls of nature from the bow or "head" of the ship), but a search being made

> for him afterwards, it was found that he had thrown himself overboard: and I was then first made acquainted with the theft and its circumstances. The loss of this man was the more regretted as he was remarkably quiet and industrious and as the very action that put an end to his life was a proof of an ingenuous mind; for to such only disgrace is insupportable.

The awful state of depression the young fellow must have been in hardly bears thinking about, for the jibes and taunts of his messmates on his sensitive mind made the oblivion of the cruel sea preferable to a moment longer in their company. It becomes doubly tragic when we realize that only a week later the monotony of the voyage was broken and if the incident had happened then it would probably have been laughed off, for the excitement of fresh experiences would have given them something else, other than bullying, to think about and the affair would have assumed its proper perspective.

Eight days after the unhappy affair, Peter Briscoe, now fully recovered from his dreadful experience at Tierra del Fuego, was one of the lookouts on the forenoon watch, and looking southward his eyes travelled over a low, scarcely discernible cloud. But could it be land? He turned his eyes away for a moment then looked afresh; it was land — no, it was a cloud. He would wait a minute then view it again, he didn't want to make a fool of himself. But now he was certain. Uncalled, it burst from his lips, "Land, LAND, land ahead!" The word flew round the ship, below deck, "Land!" and men dashed for the ladder, from the galley, the bosun's stores and paint shop. "Land!" Drop everything and scramble for the upper deck. In the wardroom Lieutenant Hicks heard it and jumped for the ladder; halfway up he realized he had forgotten his telescope and turned to collect it, but the onrush of sailors carried him up backwards. No use to shout, "Gangway for an officer," for above decks they were shouting "Land!" and officers and men were streaming to the ship's sides, feasting their eyes on that indistinct blur to the south, like men parched with thirst gulping back water. After two and a half months at sea, land; after the horrors of Cape Horn and the tantalizing boredom of Rio de Janeiro, land, lovely green land. It was good.

> To us who for a long time had seen nothing but water and sky, except the dreary hills of Tierra del Fuego, these groves seemed a terrestrial paradise.
>
> I immediately hauled up for it, and found it to be an island of an oval shape, with a lagoon in the middle, which occupied much the larger part of it.

As they approached this tiny island they could distinguish trees and natives walking among the coconuts and palms. Cook sailed to within a mile of the shore, but could find no bottom at a hundred and thirty fathoms, and so, unable to anchor, he stood out to sea again. Appropriately enough, they named it Lagoon Island.

Three hours later they made another landfall, a tiny island not much above a mile in compass. "We called it Thrumb Cap," and Cook created his own little South Sea mystery, for all other land discovered was named after its appearance, or some happening or coincidence that occurred there. It seems as though Cook deliberately gave the islands descriptive names to help future navigators to identify them. It certainly proves most helpful in this respect, for the look-outs know what to look for. It is also typical of Cook's thoughtfulness and practical mind.

> We went on with a fine trade-wind and pleasant weather, and on the 5th, about three in the afternoon, we discovered land to the westward. It proved to be a low island of much greater extent than either of those that we had seen before, being about ten or twelve leagues in compass. Several of us remained at the mast-head the whole evening, admiring its extraordinary figure; it was shaped exactly like a bow, the arc and cord of which were land, and the space between them water.

By sunset they had sailed along about half its length and Cook again attempted to anchor, but again was unable to find a bottom. Night comes on so quickly in tropical waters that within minutes of the sun's sinking below the horizon it was dark, and they completely lost sight of the island. "We steered by the sound of the breakers, which were distinctly heard, till we got clear of the coast." Their evening meals were livened now with fascinating discussions on the sights of the day and the pleasant game of naming islands. This last island "we called Bow Island." That "we" is significant of Cook's character; never "I," never a hint of boastfulness or a suggestion that but for his own superb seamanship they might still be battering their way through the Strait of Le Maire. He thought of his ship's company as a team in which even the ship's boy was an equal partner, for on more than one occasion he captioned land after the name of the lookout who first spotted it. Human nature being what it is, the men found it gratifying and a real feather in their cap to boast, on their return home, that such and such a point of land was named after them. Cook was essentially a modest man, and unbeknown to themselves his men loved him for the feeling of usefulness he gave them, a quite unique system of command for those days, when the average Captain looked upon his sailors as something from which to flog the last ounce of work.

They knew this last island to be inhabited, because of smoke which they saw in different parts, but Lieutenant Gore's imagination soared and Cook thought his story rather a tall one. "Mr. Gore, my second Lieutenant, said, after we had sailed by the island, that he had seen several of the natives, under the first clump of trees, from the deck; that he had distinguished their houses, and seen several canoes hauled up under the shade, but in this he was more fortunate than any other person on board."

The next day, however, they found more islands, naming them the Group, and had their first close-up view of the Polynesians, for, while they were again making a further unsuccessful attempt to anchor, the natives came off from the shore in canoes. In *Endeavour* all hoped that they might lure them aboard, but they failed, the natives keeping a respectful distance between themselves and the ship. That evening Cook wrote a careful note of their appearance, for we must not forget that back in England some people expected them to find a completely differently built race. Dwarfs, or giants, they did not mind which, but different they must be. The simplicity of Cook's description was equalled by its brevity and shattered the illusions of the theorist: "According to the best judgement that we could form of the people when we were nearest the shore, they were about our size and well made."

Despite the fact that they could not anchor, it would have been the simplest thing in the world for the Captain to have sent a well-armed boat ashore and satisfy his curiosity. It was probably a temptation not to, but his humanitarian instincts forbade it.

> The people [Polynesians], who kept abreast of the ship on the beach, made many signals; but whether they were intended to frighten us away or invite us on shore, it is not easy to determine: we returned them by waving our hats and shouting, and they replied by shouting again. We did not put their disposition to the test, by attempting to land; because, as the island was inconsiderable and as we wanted nothing that it could afford, we thought it imprudent as well as cruel to risk a contest in which the natives must have suffered by our superiority, merely to gratify an idle curiosity.

Every one aboard was in great spirits, the weather was fine, the sea calm and they were discovering islands at the rate of one a day.

> On the 7th, about half an hour after six in the morning we discovered another island, it looked green and pleas-

ant; it abounded with birds, we therefore gave it the name of Bird Island. . . . We saw land to the Northward. It appeared to be a double range of low, woody islands, joined together by reefs. The small islands and reefs that circumscribe the lake have the appearance of a chain, and we therefore gave it the name of Chain Island.

It is a pity the phrase "these jewels of the Southern Seas" has become so hackneyed, for the beauty of the islands defies description. They are so authentically what a South Sea island should be, so exactly as R. L. Stevenson describes them, that the writer breaks down to a simple list and asks the reader to mix the ingredients as he wishes and supply his own sauce in the form of adjectives. Every colour of the sphere is contained in varying shades on the main part of the island, blues, greens, and reds. Palm trees fringe the beaches and the sand is pure gold; around the whole a silver coral reef and above an azure sky, on all sides blue sea, breaking into frothy white surf as it meets the reef.

"We expected soon to fall in with the island where we had been directed to make our astronomical observations." All were longing to get ashore, their appetites whetted by the lovely lands they had passed.

VI

OTAHEITE

April, 1769

ABOUT one o'clock on Monday, the 10th of April the lookout thought they discerned land ahead in roughly the position Tahiti should show up, but it was so faint that by sunset the ship's company were still arguing as to whether it was cloud or land. The next morning there was no doubt that they had at last reached their destination, the island Wallis had named King George the Third Island. Light airs prevented them from making progress and the sails flapped ineffectively against the yards, while the sailors lined the ship's side gazing at the high, mountainous island and anticipating the pleasures of ladies' company ashore, for the few seamen who had visited Tahiti previously left them in little doubt of the welcome that awaited them. All that night they made little progress and the men lay awake tossing and thinking in their hammocks of the promised easy compliance of the dusky girls ashore.

On Wednesday morning they were little nearer than the previous night, but about seven o'clock a breeze sprang up and carried *Endeavour* gently shorewards. At eleven they were met by several native canoes all carrying young plantains and branches of trees; they kept a respectful distance, only a few approaching the ship. Eventually one canoe came alongside and handed up, with much gesticulating, their branches. For some time Cook was at a loss to know what they expected him to do with their presents, but hit on the happy idea of sticking the branches in the ship's rigging. This delighted the Tahitans, who came alongside, offering coconuts and fresh fruit. They learned later that the foliage was a token of peace.

All night the ship nosed her way gently inshore and the next morning anchored in Port Royal Bay. They were immediately surrounded by native canoes selling a variety of fruit, including breadfruit. Cook, with a typical eighteenth-century appreciation of food and command of words, describes the taste as "somewhat resembling that of the crumb of wheaton bread mixed with a Jerusalem artichoke." The memories of his youth and the many market days he had spent as a child, clutching his father's hand while his parent haggled over the price of a pig, sprang to his mind, the inherent carefulness of generations of peasant forebears and the hardheaded business sense of a North Countryman, drew this from him: "They had with them a pig, which they would not part with for anything but a hatchet, and therefore we refused to purchase it; because if we gave them a hatchet for a pig now, we knew they would never afterwards sell one for less, and we could not afford to buy as many as it was probable we should want at that price." Hatchets, nails or anything of metal appealed most to the Polynesians, for they were still living in a stone age. This proved a snag for Cook, but an immeasurable blessing to the seamen.

Among the natives that came to the ship the first morning

was an old man who recognized Lieutenant Gore as one of Captain Wallis' ship's company. The Second Lieutenant informed his Captain how very useful the old man had been, and Cook seized the opportunity of establishing good relations and paid particular attention to gratifying him.

But the intricacies of bargaining and the lessons of his youth continued to tug at the back of Cook's mind.

As our stay here was not likely to be very short, and as it was necessary that the merchandise which we had brought for traffic with the natives should not diminish in its value, which it would certainly have done if every person had been at liberty to give what he pleased for such things as he should purchase; at the same time, that confusion and quarrels must necessarily have arisen from there being no standard at market, I drew up the following rules, and ordered that they should be punctually observed:

Rules to be observed by every person in or belonging to His Majesty's Bark the *Endeavour,* for the better establishing of a regular and uniform trade for Provisions, etc., with the inhabitants of George's Island.

I. To endeavour, by every fair means, to cultivate a friendship with the natives, and to treat them with all imaginable humanity.

II. A proper person or persons will be appointed to trade with the natives for all manner of provisions, fruit and other production of the earth: and no officer or seaman, or other person belonging to the ship, excepting such as are so appointed, shall trade or offer to trade for

> any sort of provision, fruit or production of the earth, unless they have leave so to do.
>
> III. Every person employed on shore on any duty whatsoever, is strictly to attend to the same: and if by any neglect he loseth any of his arms, or working tools, or suffers them to be stolen, the full value thereof will be charged against his pay, according to the custom of the Navy in such cases; and he shall receive such other punishment as the nature of the offence may deserve.
>
> IV. The same penalty will be inflicted on every person who is found to embezzle, trade, or offer to trade, with any part of the ship's stores of what nature soever.
>
> V. No sort of iron or anything that is made of iron, or any sort of cloth, or other useful or necessary article, are to be given in exchange for anything but provisions.

These rules are remarkably restrained, and show an amazing simmering down of the brutal code of punishment in force at that time. If they are to be judged fairly, they should be set against the typical England and navy of the eighteenth century, which I tried to describe briefly in Chapter I.

The last rule indicates clearly how Cook's mind was unencumbered by the mushy nonsense of the "noble Savage," so freely and thirstily believed in England. Quite obviously, however noble these savages might be, he still expected to find among them the oldest profession in the world, that of prostitution. How right he was is indicated by this remark: "These people set a high value upon spike nails, yet these being an article with which many people in the ship were provided, the women found a much more easy way of procuring them than by bringing down provisions." Greatly though Cook was respected, a respect backed up by the traditions and discipline of the Royal Navy, he graciously admits the superior strength of the Polynesian whore.

As soon as the ship secured, Captain Cook, Joseph Banks, Dr. Solander, and an armed party, taken purely as a safety precaution with no intention of intimidating the natives, went ashore. They were met and welcomed by some hundreds of natives all carrying the symbolic branch. They appeared to be overwhelmed with awe, and the first Tahitan to approach crouched so low that he almost crept on hands and knees. He presented a branch and the English party were struck by the remarkable coincidence that it was the same symbol of peace known to have been in use among the ancient Greeks and Romans: the green bough of a tree. Cook considered it a diplomatic courtesy to arm himself and party with similar tokens.

Tahitans and English marched inland through the woods for about half a mile, then the natives stopped, cleared a space on the ground, and threw down their branches. Cook thought it best to follow their example: "we immediately showed our readyness to comply, and to give a greater solemnity to the rite the marines were drawn up and, marching in order, each dropped his bough upon those of the Indians." Doubtless this was done with the best intentions in the world, but it is impossible to resist the ridiculous picture of that great, bullying sergeant of the marines, the same that had driven the young soldier to suicide, complying with this unique order. Let us hope that as he sweated profusely in full uniform under a broiling tropical sun, the leaves of his offering may have tickled his nose and made him feel as stupid as he must have looked.

They continued their walk through woods which nature had laid out like a wonderland of loveliness planted with brightly coloured tropical plants; above them the trees rustled gently in the breeze, affording a welcome shade, and under foot was pleasant, springy turf, their steps unhindered by undergrowth. They found it impossible to believe that such perfection was just as it had been created; surely spirits must tend this exotic island garden; surely this was paradise.

> The shade is the most delightful that can be imagined. It consists of groves of bread-fruit and coconuts, without underwood, which are intersected, in all directions, by paths that lead from one house to the other. Nothing can be more grateful than this shade in so warm a climate, nor anything more beautiful than these walks. As there is no underwood, the shade cools without impeding the air.

It was too much after the monotonous months at sea; the natives relaxed, shaking off their first timid sense of the English superiority, they danced, sang, and delighted their guests with the charm and ease of their manner, gathering great garlands of wild flowers and festooning the sailors. Yes, even the sweating red neck of the sergeant of marines was adorned; nevertheless he was careful to shift his floral decoration slightly and allow his rank markings to shine forth.

James Cook continued his rhapsody of words at the natural beauty of Tahiti. "Our circuit was not less than four or five miles, through groves of trees, which were loaded with coconuts and breadfruit, and afforded the most grateful shade. Under these trees were the habitations of the people, most of them being only a roof without walls, and the whole scene realized the poetical fables of Arcadia." But the spirit of the farmer's boy dragged at his coattails. "All very beautiful, all very marvellous," it whispered, "something missing though, can't live on flowers." For though Cook had drunk in the loveliness of the scene, he felt bound to admit that "We remarked, however, not without some regret, that in all our walk we had seen only two hogs, and not a single fowl."

The Captain gathered from the few members of his party who were revisiting the island that he had not yet met with real aristocracy, so he determined to go back to the ship, return the next morning, and endeavour to find out the *noblesse* in their retreats.

In the morning, however, before they could leave the ship, the upper crust of Tahitan society anticipated their wishes, for the ship was surrounded by several canoes, two of which appeared to contain people of superior rank. A couple of these dignitaries were invited aboard and performed yet another welcoming ceremony by pulling off their clothes and dressing Cook and Banks in them. They were presented with beads and the established favourite, a hatchet. By their gestures they indicated they would like Cook to follow; he readily consented, hoping to combine a social call with a search for a better anchorage. Naturally enough the ever inquisitive Banks and his faithful satellite, Solander, included themselves in the party. Two boats were lowered and they set off for a point about a league to the southwest. On landing they were met by a crowd of natives numbering hundreds, and conducted to a house of much greater length than any they had seen. Here they were introduced to a middle-aged man whose name they assumed to be Tootahah, a gentleman who was to figure largely during their stay on the island. Presents were exchanged, Banks and Cook receiving a chicken apiece and a length of cloth, and Banks returned the compliment by offering his laced silk neckcloth and a linen pocket handkerchief: "Tootahah immediately dressed himself in this new finery with an air of perfect complacency and satisfaction." These ceremonies completed, the party was handed over to the women of the village for further entertainment.

They had only been a day at Tahiti, but it was becoming increasingly obvious that the easy compliance of the female population was no figment of the imagination on the part of those who had visited the island before. Cook's qualities were great and numerous and, not the least, was that of a most discerning eye for the ladies; certainly he had been close enough to them to assert positively, on paper, that their breath did not smell.

> Soon after interchanging our presents with Tootahah, they [the ladies] attended us to several large houses, in which we walked about with great freedom: they showed us all the civility of which, in our situation, we could accept; and, on their part, seemed to have no scruple that would have prevented its being carried farther. The

houses, which, as I have observed before, are all open, except the roof, afforded no place of retirement; but the ladies, by frequently pointing to the mats upon the ground, and sometimes seating themselves and drawing us down upon them, left no room to doubt of their being much less jealous of observation than we.

The Englishmen courageously withstood this siege, though there is little doubt they were impressed by the beauties of the women. Seven words sufficed to describe the men, "tall, strong, well-limbed and finely shaped," but it takes pages of Cook's closely written journal to do justice to the women. They learned that the relationship between the sexes was the all-important factor of their lives; their dances, conversation, and even their religion were based on the union of men and women. But, as Cook gallantly says,

it is now time that I should take some notice of the ladies.

The women of the superior rank are also in general above our middle stature, but those of the inferior class are rather below it. This defect in size probably proceeds from their early commerce with men, the only thing in which they differ from their superiors that could possibly affect their growth. Their natural complexion is that of a clear olive, or brunette, which many people in Europe prefer to the finest white and red — the skin is most delicately smooth and soft; they have no tint in their cheeks which we distinguish by the name colour. The shape of the face is comely, the cheek bones are not high, neither are the eyes hollow, nor the brow prominent: the only feature that does not correspond with our ideas of beauty is the nose, which, in general, is somewhat flat; but their eyes, especially those of the women, are full of expression, sometimes sparkling with fire, and sometimes melting with softness; their teeth also are, almost without exception, most beautifully even and white, and their breath perfectly without taint.

The hair is almost universally black — perfectly clean and neat. Both sexes also eradicate every hair from under their arms, and accused us of great uncleanliness for not doing the same. In their motions there is at once vigour and ease; their walk is graceful, their deportment liberal, and their behaviour to strangers and to each other affable and courteous. In their dispositions also, they seemed to be brave, open and candid, without either suspicion or treachery, cruelty or revenge; so that we place the same confidence in them as in our best friends, many of us, particularly Mr. Banks, sleeping frequently in their houses in the woods, without a companion, and, consequently, wholly in their power. They were, however, all thieves; and when that is allowed they need not much fear a competition with the people of any other nation upon earth.

In other countries the girls and unmarried women are supposed to be wholly ignorant of what others upon occasions may appear to know; and their conduct and conversation are consequently restrained within narrower bounds, and kept at a more remote distance from whatever relates to a connection with the other sex, but here it is just contrary. Among other diversions, there is a dance, called Timorodee, which is performed by the young girls, whenever eight or ten of them can be collected together, consisting of motions and gestures beyond imagination wanton, in the practice of which they are brought up from their earliest childhood, accompanied by words which, if it were possible, would more explicitly convey the same idea. In these dances they keep time with an exactness which is scarcely excelled by the best performers upon the stages of Europe. But the practice which is allowed to the virgin is prohibited to the woman from the moment that she has put these hopeful lessons in practice, and realized the symbols of the dance.

They do not sit up above an hour after dark; but when they have strangers who sleep in the house, they generally keep a light burning all night, possibly as a check upon such of the women as they do not wish to honour them with their favours.

Privacy, indeed, is little wanted among people who have not even the idea of indecency, and who gratify every appetite and passion before witnesses with no more sense of impropriety than we feel when we satisfy our hunger at a social board with our family or friends. Those who have no idea of indecency with respect to actions, can have none with respect to words; it is, therefore, scarcely necessary to observe that in the conversation of these people, that which is the principal source of their pleasure is always the principal topic, and that everything is mentioned without any restraint or emotions, and in the most direct terms, by both sexes.

It cannot be supposed that, among these people, chastity

is held in much estimation. It might be expected that sisters and daughters would be offered to strangers, either as a courtesy or for reward; and that breaches of conjugal fidelity, even in the wife, should not be otherwise punished than by a few hard words, or perhaps a slight beating, as indeed is the case; but there is a scale in dissolute sensuality, which these people have ascended, wholly unknown to every other nation whose manners have been recorded from the beginning of the world to the present hour, and which no imagination could possibly conceive.

But I must not conclude my account of the domestic life of these people without mentioning their personal cleanliness. If that which lessens the good of life and increases the evil is vice, surely cleanliness is a virtue: the want of it tends to destroy both beauty and health, and mingles disgust with our best pleasures. The natives of Otaheite [Tahiti], both men and women, constantly wash their whole bodies in running water three times every day; once as soon as they rise in the morning, once at noon, and again before they sleep at night, whether the sea or river is near them or at a distance. They wash not only the mouth but the hands at their meals, almost between every morsel; and their clothes, as well as their persons, are kept without spot or stain; so that in a large company of these people nothing is suffered but heat which, perhaps, is more than can be said of the politest assembly in Europe.

The strong desire to steal, which Cook mentions, was a decided nuisance to the English. One theft, to be mentioned later, if it had not been righted, would certainly have finished Cook's naval career in disgrace and humiliation. Yet he could write the following; but remember when reading these words that the laws of Great Britain condoned the hanging of children of eight for the theft of articles valued at twopence.

> I had given strict orders that they should not be fired upon, even when detected in these attempts [of theft], for which I had many reasons: the common sentinels were by no means fit to be entrusted with a power of life and death, to be exacted whenever they should think fit; and I had already experienced that they were ready to take away lives that were in their power upon the slightest occasion; neither, indeed, did I think that the thefts which these people committed against us were, in themselves, crimes worthy of death: that thieves are hanged in England I thought no reason why they should be shot in Otaheite; because, with respect to the natives, it would have been an execution by a law *ex post facto.* They had no such law amongst themselves, and it did not appear to me that we had any right to make such a law for them. That they should abstain from theft, or be punished with death, was not one of the conditions under which they claimed the advantage of civil society, as it is among us; and I was not willing to expose them to firearms, loaded with shot.

These quotations add up to an astounding chronicle of a human race untouched by sin, living as they had lived for thousands of years and of such a kindly nature that laws among them were scarcely necessary. Perhaps Cook sensed that in these people the eternal conflict of mind over matter did not exist, the demands of the mind and body were not at war with one another, for they accepted the commands of the flesh and executed them without shame. There was no struggle of conscience, the stronger momentary passion came first. It was a new experience for Cook. In all the societies he knew the social code expected virgins to guard their chastity till marriage, and after marriage the husband guarded his wife as a paid-for asset. The amoral islanders were unaware of this law, for in them there was little jealousy, no conception of wrong, no original sin. He saw them in their true light, he neither condemned nor condoned them; he drew no parallels as to whether their way of life or that of Europe was correct. He recorded accurately their mental outlook as far as he could ascertain it and made no attempt to alter it. He accepted their laws as stronger than those of His Majesty's government, with a brilliant clarity of the true picture, quite unrecognizable to the rest of the expedition, who thought no more of shooting a native than a dog. Cook did his utmost to leave the Tahitans as he found them and was humble enough to realize that he was no judge of right and wrong in a people who had only the slightest contact with Europeans. He even went to the extent of checking his ship's company before they landed to ascertain that there was no venereal disease among them. In this he was too late, for either Wallis or Bougainville had already contaminated the natives.

He saw, and recorded in a unique document, a brief glimpse of a few months into a life never before known and soon to be shattered by the slimy hands of Europe. It was as if he had lifted a coffin lid and glimpsed for a second the dead face of the corpse before it disintegrated in dust, for within Cook's lifetime the Tahitans were reduced to a mouldering, decadent, and diseased race. Exploited and ruined by the enlightened hand of Europe, taught to sin in order to be taught not to sin, taught that their beautiful, naked, athletic bodies were things to be covered up and be ashamed of, as indeed they were by the time Europe had poxed the race from top to bottom.

Cook could only hint at the reasons for this perfect state, suggesting that the absence of the necessity to work might account for their happy dispositions. "The earth produced spontaneously, or with so little culture, that they seemed to be exempted from the first general curse that 'man should eat his bread in the sweat of his brow.' "

There they were, a finely made, healthy, clean race, possessed with a happy, open disposition and a natural kindness and courteousness towards each other. But, as a man not injected against smallpox is likely to suffer the full ravages of the disease if it attacks him, so in their case the Tahitans had no antitoxins of evil in their make-up; anything so beautiful is bound to be brittle. They soaked up the inky filth of Europe like clean blotting-paper: the educated, cultured North unconcernedly trampled to death the only bit of heaven left on earth. It was disgraceful and sad, terribly, terribly sad.

The last few pages have been a necessary digression from the story to show the type of people and country in which the observations of Venus were to be made. It also brings out forcibly another side of Cook's character, for to his other qualities must now be added that of philosopher. The deep, gentle kindliness and decency of his treatment of the childlike Tahitans earns him that title.

We left the Captain, Banks, and the party bravely withstanding a delightful female siege. They realized that retreat was the only answer to the charming overtures. Reluctantly they took leave of the friendly chief and continued their walk along the beach. After covering about a mile they met another chief, Toubourai Tamaide, at the head of a great number of people. This time Captain Cook unhesitatingly went through the greeting ceremonies and embellished his actions with the word "Taio" which he supposed to signify "friend." This chief gave them to understand that if they chose to eat he had victuals ready for them.

> We accepted his offer, and dined very heartily upon fish, bread-fruit, coconuts and plantains, dressed after their manner: they ate some of their fish raw, and a raw fish was offered to us, but we declined that part of the entertainment.

Once again women complicated matters, Banks figuring in the eternal triangle of love; and for the first time they experienced the light fingers of the islanders.

> During this visit a wife of our noble host, whose name was Tomio, did Mr. Banks the honour to place herself upon the same mat, close by him. Tomio was not in the

> first bloom of her youth, nor did she appear to have been ever remarkable for her beauty; he did not, therefore, I believe, pay her the most flattering attention: it happened, too, as a further mortification to this lady, that seeing a very pretty girl among the crowd he, not adverting to the dignity of his companion, beckoned her to come to him: the girl, after some entreaty, complied, and sat down on the other side of him: he loaded her with beads and every showy trifle that would please her: his princess, though she was somewhat mortified at the preference that was given her rival, did not discontinue her civilities, but still assiduously supplied him with the milk of the coconut, and such other dainties as were in her reach. This scene might possibly have become more curious and interesting if it had not been suddenly interrupted by an interlude of a more serious kind.

Solander and Monkhouse had no objection to one caressing female arm around their shoulders, in fact they liked it, encouraged it, but they objected strongly to the other dusky limb's exploring their pockets. On discovering that nimble fingers had dexterously removed an opera glass in a shagreen case from Dr. Solander, and from Mr. Monkhouse his snuffbox, they complained to the chief. "This incident unfortunately put an end to the good humour of the company." Banks flung off the encumbering arms around him and, giving the complaint weight, jumped to his feet, hastily striking the butt end of his firelock on the ground. The effect of this noisy demonstration was instantaneous, every one of the natives ran out of the house with the utmost precipitation, except the chief and two or three others who appeared by their dress to be of superior rank.

In a desperate attempt to atone for the wrong which had been done, the chief took Banks by the hand, offering him, piece by piece, a large quantity of cloth, but Banks was not to be bribed and intimated by signs that the stolen property was all he wanted. In despair the chief rushed out and left Banks to the unwelcome advances of the ugly princess; unfortunately his beauty queen had been frightened away by the firelock. In about half an hour the chief returned with the stolen goods, his face transported with joy, a joy that melted into horror when, on opening the case, the opera glass was found to be missing. This time they all rushed out and eventually the opera glass was recovered. It was only a trifling incident, but sufficient to impress on Cook the influence the chiefs wielded. An "influence which would do honour to any system of government."

Their goods recovered, the English made tracks for the ship, tired out with the diversity of their experiences on the first full day ashore; overwhelmed and shattered by the women, and filled with a pleasant expectancy of the joys that lay ahead.

"In the evening, about six o'clock, we returned to the ship."

VII

MORE OF OTAHEITE

April–July, 1769

COOK now settled down to the serious work of building a fort to be used as a base for the observation. He selected a sandy beach locked by a fresh-water stream, with the additional advantage of being some distance from native houses. With the help of Banks he pegged out the plan, but they were soon surrounded by a crowd of curious Tahitans. However, they seemed perfectly satisfied to sit outside a ring the Captain marked in the sand, and allow the English to work unmolested. They "behaved with a deference and respect that at once pleased and surprised us." Their only concern seemed to be to prevent the sailors from penetrating inland and Cook suspected that the much needed pigs had been driven farther into the country.

The survey took about two hours and after its completion the Captain and Banks determined to walk a little way in search of hogs, leaving behind a guard of thirteen marines in charge of a petty officer.

They walked half a mile through pleasant woods when Banks, without warning or tact, fired at some duck, killing three with one shot, surprising himself and terrifying the natives, who flung themselves face down on the ground. They were barely recovered from their fright when a further shot rang out from the fort. Thoroughly alarmed Cook rushed back to the stockade. His worst fears were confirmed, for the petty officer informed him that a native had attempted to grab a sentry's rifle. With complete contempt for life, the party had fired point-blank into a crowd of a hundred natives, who had fled in terror. Not satisfied with that, and noticing the thief still alive, they gave chase and shot him dead in cold blood. The marines fell back before the blazing fury of their Captain, trying desperately to justify the action by elaborating their story, armed men hoping to convince Cook that they had been "violently assaulted and thrown down" by a single unarmed native. A great bitterness and loathing filled him as he tried to justify their action to the Tahitans; his eyes clouded with pity for these people who "went away without any appearance of distrust or resentment." Then he turned to the petty officer, his words cut through his excuses like a lash, accusing him of firing "perhaps from a sudden fear of further violence, perhaps from the natural petulance of power newly acquired, and perhaps from a brutality in his nature." And to the marines, who had shown "as little consideration or humanity as the officer."

The next day it was obvious that the incident had greatly upset the Tahitans, for there were only a few on the beach instead of the usual hundreds; the men missed more than they liked to admit the friendly smile and cheerful greetings of the natives as they paddled swiftly to the ship's side to barter fresh fruit. Cook went ashore in the evening but was sad to detect a distinct difference in their attitude. Nevertheless, his orders were to observe the transit of Venus, whatever the temper of the islanders, and he considered it a necessary precaution to warp the ship nearer to the beach, covering the proposed site of the fort with his guns.

As if by a strange justice of fate, a reprisal for the taking of an innocent life, Mr. Buchan, the artist, died the next day.

> He had always been subject to epileptic fits, one of which seized him on the mountains of Tierra del Fuego; and this disorder being aggravated by a bilious complaint which he contracted on board ship, at length put an end to his life. . . . He was a sober, diligent and ingenious young man.

It seems extraordinary that anyone was allowed to embark on the voyage in such a state of health. The other artist, Mr. Parkinson, carried on the important task under scarcely ideal conditions. Flies "made it almost impossible to work; for they not only covered his subject so that no part of its surface could be seen, but even ate the colour off the paper as fast as he could lay it on."

They buried Buchan at sea in deference to any scruples or suspicions the Tahitans might have at witnessing a strange ceremony, for Monkhouse, the surgeon, had found the body of the shot native, lying on a raised bier in an appalling state of decomposition, though placed not more than ten yards from dwelling houses. He would have examined it more closely "but for the stench of the body, which was intolerable." The practice of allowing their dead to rot above ground seemed the only unpleasant characteristic found among the Polynesians.

The building of the fortifications continued, Cook sparing every man possible from the ship and endeavouring to restore good relations with the natives, with a fair measure of success, for now they were not content to watch the seamen work, but insisted on helping. He returned this goodwill and "purchased every stake that was used upon this occasion, and cut down no tree till we had first obtained their consent." Provisions of breadfruit, coconut, even hogs rolled in and for the first time since arriving at Tahiti, "we served fresh pork to the ship's company."

The combined fort and observatory was completed well in advance of June 3, the day of the transit of Venus. In the afternoon of Monday, the 1st of May, the quadrant, an indispensable instrument for the observation, was taken in its packing-case and placed in the Captain's tent under armed guard. The following morning the two astronomers, Cook and Green, went ashore to experiment with their precious instrument, but on entering the tent they discovered to their inexpressible horror and concern that the packing-case was missing. Every conceivable solution rushed through Cook's mind; it had accidentally been taken back to the ship; one of the seamen had stolen it, thinking it contained nails or something else useful for bartering. That it might have been stolen by the natives hardly entered his mind, for the box was heavy and an armed sentry had stood outside the tent all night. His whole naval career depended on finding the quadrant; he had been sent thousands of miles to this distant island, at a vast expense to his country, specifically to observe Venus; he had sailed halfway round the world for Venus, but the loss of that little box, measuring eighteen inches square, meant ruin, disgrace and humiliation for Lieutenant Cook. "Without this, we could not perform the service for which our voyage was principally undertaken." He approached near to panic, and offered a large reward to anyone who found it, supposing the box to have been stolen by one of his sailors and hoping that a bribe might induce the thief to produce it. But it was not forthcoming. The fort was turned upside down, still no box; the ship was searched from stem to stern without result, and an appalling apprehension began to build in his mind, that, despite all precautions, the natives were the culprits. The solemn words of the Admiralty's sailing orders churned through his brain with maddening intensity: "observe the passage of the planet Venus over the disk of the sun — taking care, however, not to suffer yourself to be surprised by the natives, but to be always upon your guard against any accident." He could not observe the transit of Venus through the very contingency the Admiralty had anticipated in their strongly worded warning.

To find the quadrant among the natives presented an almost impossible solution; there were thousands of Tahitans, and a thief who had risked death to steal the box could not be expected to return it willingly. Joseph Banks proved a loyal friend, for he had more influence over the natives than any of them, and immediately made off for the woods, accompanied only by Green and a midshipman. Half despairingly Cook watched his youthful figure disappear in the forest, resigning himself to a long, probably unfruitful, wait.

Banks pressed forward, sometimes walking, sometimes running, though the weather was intolerably hot. As he was crossing a river he met Toubourai Tamaide, the influential chief known to him, who immediately made the figure of a triangle with three bits of straw on his hand. By this, Banks knew that the natives were the thieves and had opened the packing-case. No time was to be lost. He made Tamaide understand that he must go with him and guide him to wherever the quadrant had been carried. They set out together, the chief enquiring after the thief by name at every house they passed. The people told him readily enough which way he had gone and how long it was since he had been there. Banks, Green, the midshipman, and the native chief ran stumbling on for four miles, the clothes of the Englishmen sticking to their bodies, their legs aching with tiredness, and sweat ran stinging into their eyes. Eventually they reached the top of a hill. Tamaide stopped and pointed to a spot a good three miles farther on, giving them to understand that that was where the quadrant would be found. Gasping for breath Banks reviewed the situation. They had no arms except a pair of pistols he always carried in his pocket, they were going to a place at least seven miles from the fort, where the natives might be less submissive, to take from them an article they had risked their lives to get and did not seem anxious to surrender. Obviously the dangers of their situation would become more critical with every step they ventured farther inland.

Banks bravely determined that he and Green should go on, sending the midshipman back with the information and a request to Cook to follow as soon as possible with a party of men. They pursued their journey deeper into the unknown forest, accompanied by Tamaide, and in the very spot he had specified met one of the natives with a part of the quadrant in his hand. Banks could have wept for joy, but there was little time to give vent to his emotions, for in a matter of minutes they were surrounded by a great number of natives, a crowd that increased rapidly to several hundred, pressing in roughly upon the two solitary Englishmen, with gestures and growls that were anything but friendly. There were two alternatives before Banks, either to try and pacify them, or have a show of strength and produce a pistol. He knew how piteously small his demonstration of strength might prove. If the pistol incited the natives he had two shots, perhaps two killed out of a hostile crowd of nearly a thousand islanders; the inevitable onrush, a few seconds of exquisite agony as they clubbed and tore the Englishmen to mincemeat, then oblivion. . . . Here lay the remains of Joseph Banks and Charles Green. . . . He whipped out his pistol, waiting tensely for their reaction, the back of his neck tingling as he watched their faces, the hungry cruel glitter of their eyes. The angry grumbling softened, died away, and for a moment there was silence; then they fell back, subdued. The thousand-to-one chance had come off, the daring rashness of his bluff worked. They breathed again and Banks slipped his pistol back into his pocket, concealing his hand for a minute to hide its trembling. Quickly he drew a circle around them on the ground; a great quietness had come over the crowd and they stayed outside the mark. The precious box was placed in the middle of the circle and Green impatiently tore off the lid. It was all there except for a few small things, but Banks now had the upper hand and in a few minutes the odd gadgets were returned. They set off back for the fort and after about two miles met Cook and his party, scarcely able to contain their relief at the sight of the box. "We congratulated each other upon the recovery of the quadrant, with a pleasure proportionate to the importance of the event."

A few days before the transit, Cook sent two parties to different points to make additional observations. The 3rd of June proved a perfect day, "there not being a cloud in the sky from the rising to the setting of the sun, the whole passage of the planet Venus over the sun's disk was observed with great advantage by Mr. Green, Dr. Solander and myself." They were all delighted, but unfortunately, on their return to England, the observations were useless, for the results from Norway and the Hudson Bay were hopelessly inaccurate.

Cook had successfully accomplished the first part of his orders, but between the theft of the quadrant and the observation, a month had elapsed — a month of intense interest during which they had learned a great deal about the Tahitans, their food, their customs, pleasures, sports, and pastimes. They had many adventures, some exciting, some sad and some hilariously funny. They made firm friends of the natives and learned how close to the surface their passions were, expressions flitting across their faces like fast-moving shadows, tears that could turn from joy to remorse or anger in seconds. The islanders' incredible, cunning ability for theft.

> I must bear my testimony that the people of this country, of all ranks, men and women, are the arrantest thieves

> upon the face of the earth. The very day after we arrived here, when they came on board us, the Chiefs were employed in stealing what they could in the cabin, and their dependants were no less industrious in other parts of the ship; they snatched up everything that it was possible for them to secrete till they got on shore, even to the glass ports, two of which they carried off undetected.

It was never discovered how they managed to steal the quadrant, but for ingenuity this episode takes some beating:

> In the middle of the night, one of the natives contrived to steal an iron coal-rake, that was made use of for the oven. It happened to be set up against the inside of the wall, so that the top of the handle was visible from without: and we were informed that the thief who had been lurking there in the evening, came secretly about three o'clock in the morning and watching his opportunity when the sentinel's back was turned, very dexterously laid hold of it with a long crooked stick, and drew it over the wall.

Cook adequately summed up this vice. "That they are thieves is true, but as among these people, no man can be much injured or benefited by theft, it is not necessary to restrain it by such punishments as in other countries are absolutely necessary to the very existence of civil society." By experience Cook discovered that the best way to ensure the return of stolen goods was to confiscate the natives' fishing canoes until his own property was returned.

Inevitably, the English sailors were not wholly blameless, in regard to stealing either from the Tahitans or the ship's stores. The first serious incident occurred one evening, after Tamaide, with several other chiefs, had dined at the fort. Shortly after taking his leave from the English, he rushed back in a state of great emotion, imploring Banks to follow him into the woods. Banks immediately complied, and soon found the ship's butcher with a reaping hook in his hand. The chief, in a transport of rage, made it understood that the butcher had taken a fancy to a stone hatchet, offering his wife a nail in exchange. The lady was unwilling to part with it for that price, whereupon the butcher threatened to cut her throat unless his wishes were gratified. The offender had little to say in his defense and Banks promised that if found guilty he should be punished.

The next time Tamaide visited the ship Cook took the opportunity of calling up the butcher, convinced himself of his guilt and ordered flogging. Fascinated, the natives watched the defaulter stripped and lashed to the rigging and with a fixed attention they followed every movement of the master-at-arms. Dipping his cat-o'-nine-tails in a bucket of water, he drew the wet thongs gently through his hand, choosing with a professional eye the first target of flesh. They waited in silent suspense as the lash was drawn back, as it whistled through the air and sank into the man's back. His breath escaped in a hiss and the natives jumped up, imploring that the rest of the punishment might be remitted. "For many reasons I could not consent, and when they found they could not prevail by their intercessions, they gave vent to their pity by tears."

Cook dealt firmly and swiftly with any interference to the natives, or tampering with ship's stores. "Complaint being made to me by some of the natives that two of the seamen had taken from them several bows and arrows and some strings of plaited hair, I examined the matter, and finding the charge well supported, I punished each of the criminals with two dozen lashes."

While the officers were engrossed in the actual transit of Venus, some of the ship's company stole a hundredweight of nails. "One of the thieves was detected, but only seven nails were found in his custody. He was punished with two dozen lashes, but would impeach none of his accomplices." This seems harsh treatment, but in fact, with a man's guilt for a theft established, it was the minimum punishment Cook was allowed to give.

Always, if the Tahitans witnessed the punishment of a man who had wronged them, their tears of rage turned to those of anguish the moment the first stroke was laid on. Their tears were like those of children, ready to express any passion that excited them strongly, and like children's were forgotten as soon as shed. Banks witnessed a remarkable instance of their fleeting passions.

> Very early in the morning, even before it was day, a great number of them came down to the fort, and Terapo being observed amongst the women on the outside of the gate, Mr. Banks went out and brought her in; he saw that the tears then stood in her eyes and as soon as she entered they began to flow in great abundance: he enquired earnestly the cause, but instead of answering she took from

> under her garments a shark's tooth, and struck it six or seven times into her head with great force; a profusion of blood followed, and she talked loud, but in a most melancholy tone for some minutes, without at all regarding his enquiries, which he repeated with still more impatience and concern, while the other Indians, to his great surprise, talked and laughed without taking the least notice of her distress. But her own behaviour was still more extraordinary. As soon as the bleeding was over, she looked up with a smile and began to collect some small pieces of cloth, which during her bleeding she had thrown down to catch the blood: as soon as she had picked them all up she carried them out of the tent and threw them into the sea, carefully dispensing them abroad as if she wished to prevent the sight of them from reviving the remembrance of what she had done. She then plunged into the river and after having washed her whole body, returned to the tents with the same gaiety and cheerfulness as if nothing had happened.

There were few incidents to mar the friendly relations between English and Tahitan. Indeed it would have been difficult not to get on with such open, pleasant people. The ladies were only too pleased to gratify the sailors, and among the men a priest named Tupia became an especial friend, frequently expressing a desire to accompany *Endeavour* when she sailed. One difficulty the islanders encountered was in pronouncing British names. They therefore substituted sounds resembling as closely as possible the English counterpart. Mr. Hicks became Hete; Molineux, the Master, they renounced in absolute despair and called him Boba, from his Christian name Robert; Dr. Solander, Torano; and Banks, Tapane. A native princess did Cook no great service, considering the dignity of his position as Captain, by fondly calling him Toote, a delightful name for a muscular, weatherbeaten six-footer and a source of continual amusement to his ship's company. Cook's gallantry rose to the occasion. In return he said: "she appeared to have been handsome when she was young, but at this time little more than memorials of her beauty were left."

In the matter of eating the British stood abashed in profound respect at the colossal amounts the Tahitans stowed away, for Englishmen of the eighteenth century were no mean gormandizers themselves.

> The quantity of food which these people eat at a meal is prodigious. I have seen one man devour two or three fishes as big as a perch; three bread-fruit, each bigger than two fists; fourteen or fifteen plantains, each of them six or seven inches long, and four or five round; and near a quart of the pounded bread-fruit, which is as substantial as the thickest, unbaked custard. This is so extraordinary that I scarcely expect to be believed; and I would not have related it upon my own single testimony, but Mr. Banks, Dr. Solander and most of the other gentlemen have had ocular demonstration of its truth.

The effects of these large repasts can be imagined. "After meals, and in the heat of the day, the middle-aged people of the better sort generally sleep: they are indeed extremely indolent; and sleeping and eating is almost all they do. . . . Boys and girls are kept awake by the natural activity and sprightliness of their age."

They always ate in complete silence, the women after the men, though aboard *Endeavour* the girls "retired to the servant's apartments and ate of plantains very heartily; a mystery of female economy here, which none of us could explain." But as time passed the sailors obviously managed to overcome these delicate scruples. "When any of us have been alone with a woman she has sometimes eaten in our company; but then she has expressed the greatest unwillingness that it should be known."

One Polynesian delicacy the Englishmen particularly appreciated was cooked dog, which they thought quite as good as mutton, but perhaps it was a long time since they had eaten any. The dog was killed by holding the hands over its mouth and nose, suffocating it to death, an operation that took over quarter of an hour. Then a hole was dug in the ground about a foot deep, a fire kindled, and the dog singed by holding it over the fire, "scraping him with a shell, the hair was taken off as clean as if he had been scalded in hot water: he was then cut up with the same instrument and his entrails being taken out, were sent to the sea, where being carefully washed, they were put in a coconut shell with what blood had come from the body." Everything was placed in the hole, covered up and allowed to cook for four hours, when the dog was "taken out excellently baked; and we all agreed he made a very good dish."

Unhappily, *Endeavour's* visit to Tahiti was nearly over, but it would be inexcusable to leave the island without relating some of the weird and amusing incidents that affected the ship's company. They are not important, are unconnected with each other, and luckily have no moral. They are best grouped together as "Stories from the Captain's Journal."

Banks's Breeches

A party of six from the ship made an expedition inland to buy hogs; they were not too successful in their bargaining, but dined well with the natives, finally deciding to spend the night in the village. Banks considered himself honoured and fortunate in being offered accommodation in a Tahitan princess's canoe. He went to rest early, taking off all his clothes as was his constant practice, his princess insisting that she be allowed to guard them in case of theft, and with the rashness of youth, Banks complied. Awakening about an hour before midnight he decided to take a short stroll, but on reaching for his clothes found them missing; only his breeches remained. In great indignation he roused the princess. Equally alarmed she rushed off into the forest, but soon returned without the clothes. Banks had no idea where the rest of the party were sleeping, so thought it best for his dignity as an Englishman to fake unconcern and finish his night's rest. As can be supposed, his sleep was not very sound, and the noise of music about midnight thoroughly roused him. He decided that where there was gaiety there would be his friends, and making his way through the forest guided by the sounds of music, soon discovered Cook and three other gentlemen in a hut.

He made up to us more than half naked and told us his melancholy story. We gave him such comfort as the unfortunate generally give to each other, by telling him that

> we were fellow-sufferers; I showed him that I was myself without stockings, they having been stolen from under my head, though I was sure I had never been asleep, and each of my associates convinced him, by his appearance, that he had lost a jacket. We determined, however, to hear out the concert, however deficient we might appear in our dress . . . having agreed that nothing could be done towards the recovery of our things till the morning.

But they never found their clothes; Banks was compensated by his princess, who wrapped him in her own robes, "so that when he came up to us he made a most motley appearance, half Indian and half English."

The Dying Chief

Word was brought to the fort that a chief was dying in great agony because of something the English had given him to eat; he vomited continually, and his servants had carefully preserved a sample of this in a leaf. Banks set out immediately and "found his Indian friend leaning his head against a post, in an attitude of the utmost languor and despondency." Upon examining the contents of the leaf it was found to contain nothing but a chew of tobacco; the chief had noticed the sailors kept it in their mouths a long time and "being desirous of doing the same, he had chewed it to a powder and swallowed the spittle." During the examination of the leaf and its contents he looked up at Mr. Banks with the most piteous aspect and intimated that he had a very short time to live. A copious dose of coconut milk restored the chief to health and happiness.

A New Word for the English Dictionary

One day they saw an operation performed on a girl of about thirteen; the instrument used had thirty teeth and was struck at least a hundred times a minute into her back. The girl bore it with stoical resolution for about a quarter of an hour, but then the pain of so many hundreds of punctures became too much and she implored the operator to stop, first in murmurs, then weeping, and finally in screams. He continued unmoved. As she began to struggle two women held her down, sometimes soothing her, but when she became unruly giving her a smart blow. Banks watched the gruesome performance for over an hour and the operation was not over when he went away. The arches of the loins, the most painful part of all, were still to be done. The natives called this "tattooing."

A Unique Salute

Three pieces of cloth were laid on the ground, "the foremost of the women stepped on them and taking up her garments all round her to the waist, turned around with great composure and deliberation, and with an air of perfect innocence and simplicity, three times . . . immediately after this the cloth was rolled up and given to Mr. Banks as a present."

In Cook's journal there are many more amusing stories, which in themselves would fill a book. They watched the islanders' crude form of a boxing match, watched them throwing the javelin and surf riding in such huge seas that Cook was convinced it would have been "impossible for any

European boat to live in it; and if the best swimmer in Europe had, by any accident, been exposed to its fury, I am confident he would not have been able to preserve himself from drowning." Yet the natives sported for hours in the surf.

They learned something of the island surgery, crude in the extreme, judging from some of the dreadful scars they sometimes noticed. "We saw one man whose face was almost entirely destroyed, his nose, including the bone, was perfectly flat, and one cheek and one eye were so beaten in that the hollow would almost receive a man's fist. Another man's body had been pierced right through, from back to breast." Superstition ruled their healing: "if he recovers, they say the remedy cured him, if he dies, they say the disease was incurable; in which they do not much differ from the custom of other countries." The men found traces of previous European visitors, for within five days of arriving one of the seamen contracted venereal disease, but native superstitions and charms were powerless against this curse.

There was nothing further to detain *Endeavour* at Tahiti; the first part of the orders had been successfully carried out and they began to prepare for sea, taking in fresh water, fruit, and meat. The carpenters were busy ashore pulling down the fort for firewood on board the ship, surrounded by flocks of natives clearly showing their sorrow at the signs of departure, a sorrow shared by the English and for two young marines, too strong to resist . . . they deserted. "They had strongly attached themselves to two girls, and it was their intention to conceal themselves till the ship sailed, and take up their residence on the island."

Cook was determined to recover the men, even delaying his sailing date a day in the hopes of their return, for he wanted at all cost to avoid friction with the natives, realizing that without their goodwill it would be impossible to find the marines. But the Tahitans had accepted the deserters as being of themselves, and showed no inclination to help in the search. Finally the Captain was forced to hold several chiefs as hostages until his men were found, and within a few hours an armed party were led to their hideout. Amid hostile signs of strong disapproval by the natives the two young deserters were dragged from the arms of their lovers to the certainty of the lash. Setting the peaceful island beauty and lovely girls against the certain hardships and rough living ahead, it was incredible that more men did not desert. Nevertheless, the feeling was there, for midshipman Matra did his utmost to persuade the other two snotties to desert.

From now on no one was allowed ashore, but the day before they sailed the priest, Tupia, again asked to be taken on board. Without hesitation Cook accepted, knowing him to be a good navigator, well acquainted with the islands for some distance around, besides being useful as an interpreter. He was taken aboard with a boy of about thirteen as his servant. The next day between eleven and twelve, they weighed anchor, and as soon as the ship was under sail the natives on board left; they wept "with a decent and silent sorrow, in which there was something very striking and tender." It was sufficient to make many of the sailors swallow hard and brush their roughened hands unashamedly over their eyes. "Thus we took leave of Otaheite and its inhabitants, after a stay of just over three months, for much the greater part of the time we lived together in the most cordial friendship."

Years later, Cook realized that the Tahitans had looked upon him as a god; a fulfilment of an ancient Polynesian folk story that from the East a great white god would visit them (and as Thor Heyerdahl's *Kon-Tiki* voyage proved, a fable based on the truth of their own origin and passed down among them for hundreds of years).

VIII

INTO THE UNKNOWN

July–October, 1769

After leaving Tahiti Cook sailed among the neighbouring islands for a month, allowing his ship's company to shake down again after the debaucheries of the land of Venus, and no doubt waiting for better weather in the Southern Hemisphere, where it was winter. Light breezes prevented their making much progress, but whenever the wind freshened Tupia took full credit for it.

> Our Indian friend, Tupia, often prayed for a wind to his God Tane, and as often boasted of his success, which indeed he took a very effectual method to secure, for he never began his address to Tane till he saw a breeze so near that he knew it must reach the ship before his orison was well over.

Cook named the group of islands the Societies, and landed on several of them despite Tupia's warning that "if we remained here, they would certainly come down tomorrow and fight us. We determined, therefore, to go on shore without delay." They found the natives differed in one thing only from the Tahitans — they were even more idle, for Banks tried to gain their assistance as guides "yet they are so lazy that he could not persuade any of them to go up the hills with him; they said if they were to attempt it, the fatigue would kill them." They were, however, uncommonly skilful thieves and the dusky maidens were quite as beautiful and just as ready with their favours; "these girls seemed attentive to nothing but how to oblige us." They danced with the same rhythmic, tempting abandon.

> They advanced sideways in a measured step, keeping excellent time to the drums, which beat briskly and loud; soon after they began to shake their hips, giving the folds of cloth that lay upon them a very quick motion which was in some degree continued through the whole dance, though the body was thrown into various postures, sometimes resting on their knees and elbows, the fingers also being moved at the same time with a quickness scarcely to be imagined. Much of the dexterity of the dances, however, and the entertainment of the spectators, consisted in the wantonness of their attitudes and gestures which was indeed such as exceeds description.

The English enjoyed their visit, eating, sleeping, exchanging presents and names with the natives, one chief being delighted with the splendid new title of "King Cookee," and of course, the over-inquisitive Banks continued to investigate everything he could lay hands on with an inexcusable lack of tact. He knew the dead were revered by the Polynesians, for he had assisted in a funeral ceremony at Tahiti, yet, on finding a corpse wrapped in matting, he overcame the appalling stench sufficiently to examine it

> by putting his hand into it, and found a parcel about five feet long and one thick, wrapped up in mats; he broke a way through several of these mats with his fingers, but at length came to one which was made of the fibres of the coconut, so firmly plaited together that he found it impossible to tear it, and therefore was forced to desist, especially as he perceived that what he had done already gave great offence to our new friends.

He did, however, solve one island mystery that had puzzled them even at Tahiti: they frequently found numbers of jaw-bones tied to walls or hung on canoes. To one was "tied eight human jaw-bones; we learnt that these, like scalps among the Indians of North America, were trophies of war."

Cook took possession of the Society Islands in the name of King George, using a simple but effective method of ensuring that any future European visitors would know England was first there. He gave the chief a small pewter plate stamped with this inscription: "His Britannic Majesty's ship *Endeavour,* Lieutenant Cook, Commander, 16th July, 1769, Huaheine" (the native name of the island), relying on the promise of the chief to guard the plate with his life.

The usual trading continued, Cook buying as many hogs, fowls, and plantains as possible, especially the latter, for they found that by boiling them they could make a useful substitute for bread . . . and they needed one. "Our own bread was so full of vermin that, notwithstanding all possible care, we had sometimes twenty of them in our mouths at a time, every one of which tasted as hot as mustard."

Trading could, on occasions, be a delightful pastime. One chief "sent three very pretty girls to demand something in return for his present; perhaps he was unwilling to trust himself on board the ship, or perhaps he thought his messengers would procure a more valuable return for his hogs and poultry than he could himself; be that as it may, we did not regret his absence, nor his messengers their visit." That particular chief had a great reputation for his power, possessions, and fighting qualities, for he was the terror of all the other islands, and though Cook had never met him, he imagined him to be a vigorous, intelligent young chief and he appreciated the kindness which prompted him to send along the lovely maidens. The Captain was sadly mistaken. "We found a poor, feeble wretch withered and decrepit, half blind with age, and so sluggish and stupid that he appeared scarcely to have understanding enough left to know that it was probable we should be gratified either by hogs or women."

But the old chief had the last laugh, for the hogs he sold them would not eat, and died, and the poultry were "seized with a disease that affected the head so that they continued to hold it down between their legs till they died." Regretfully farmer Cook watched the livestock perish, but his ship's company remained healthy, with only a few occasional symptoms of scurvy, quickly cured, instead of the hitherto normal, appalling death toll.

While cruising among the Society Islands, *Endeavour* came very near to disaster when her bottom was almost torn off on a coral reef. The incident shows clearly the constant danger they were always exposed to in uncharted waters, in a small ship largely at the mercy of the wind, for however skilful the captain might be, alterations of course to avoid hidden dangers cannot be effected with anything like the speed of a powered boat with propellers to help. It was Cook's constant precaution when passing through gaps in the reefs to have his Master (the most expert and trusted mariner aboard) taking frequent soundings of the depth of water, thus obtaining forewarning of shallower water ahead. In normal seas this worked well, for the Captain would receive soundings indicating a gradual rise in the sea bed, but among the Society Islands the coral reefs rise sheer as a wall and the Captain might receive in two consecutive soundings "no bottom," completely safe, to "three fathoms," critically dangerous with only four feet of water under the ship. Cook underwent an even worse experience than this, passing through a gap.

> I was unexpectedly in the most imminent danger of striking on the rocks; the Master, who I had ordered to keep continually sounding in the chains, suddenly called out "two fathoms" [twelve feet]. This alarmed me, for though I knew the ship drew at least fourteen feet, and that therefore it was impossible such a shoal should be under her keel, yet the Master was either mistaken or she went along the edge of a coral rock.

The Master was not mistaken and for a few agonizing minutes *Endeavour* hovered alongside the razor-sharp rocks, then mercifully answered the helm and slid slowly away from her certain executioner.

Alone in his cabin Cook reread again the final, secret part of his instruction: "There is reason to believe that a continent, or land of great extent, may be found to the southwards of the tracts of former navigators — you are to proceed southward in order to make discovery of the continent above mentioned." He carefully replaced the papers in their packet, deciding that any further pretense at secrecy about their future mission was unjustified so far as his men were concerned; it was better that they know the truth, far better than allowing wild rumours and ignorant superstitions to circulate and breed discontent.

The bosun's pipe trilled out its orders: "Clear lower deck, hands to muster aft." Quietly, unemotionally, the Captain told his ship's company what lay ahead, promising a gallon of rum to the man that first sighted the great, unknown continent. The helmsman was given his course, the sails filled, the bows pointed south, and the Yorkshire coal boat, with less than a hundred men aboard and the promise of a gallon of rum, began her dramatic, history-making voyage into the unknown.

Is it possible to inject oneself into the minds of those few dozen men? Imagine their feelings when alone, high aloft in the whistling riggings, searching, searching, always search- the limitless, grey rolling expanse of the mighty unconquerable Pacific for that telltale wisp of cloud that might herald Terra Australis; huge as all the known world, mysterious as the stars.

> We sailed from Oteroah [one of the Society Islands] on the 15th August, and on Friday the 25th we celebrated the anniversary of our leaving England by taking a Chesh-

> ire cheese from the locker, where it had been carefully treasured up for this occasion, and tapping a cask of porter, which proved to be very good, and in excellent order. On the 29th, one of the sailors got so drunk that next morning he died.

For two and a half weeks they sailed south, running into ever worsening weather, then,

> there not being any signs of land, with a heavy sea from the westward, and strong gales, I wore, and stood back to the northward, fearing that we might receive such damage to our sails and rigging, as would hinder the prosecution of the voyage. On the next day, there being strong gales, to the westward, I brought to, with the ship's head to the northward; but in the morning of the 3rd, the wind being more moderate, we loosened the reef of the main-sail, set the top-sail, and plied to the westward.

Then, for five long weeks they sailed westward in long, slow tacks, kept slightly northward of 40° south by the blustering "roaring forties."

Cook's journal runs into many thousands of words, using pages and pages to describe some amusing incident, but those seven anxious weeks take little over a page. Brief, terse sentences, indicating with startling clarity the tense, suppressed excitement aboard. Many times they thought they saw land, many theories and scraps of evidence were taken as certain indications of land ahead.

> On the 24th, we observed a small piece of seaweed, and a piece of wood covered with barnacles.

On the 27th, we saw a seal asleep upon the water, and several bunches of seaweed. The next day we saw more seaweed in bunches.

On the 29th, a bird, which we thought a land bird.

On the 1st October, we saw birds, innumerable, and another seal asleep upon the water; it is a general opinion that seals never go out of soundings, or far from land, but those that we saw in these seas prove the contrary. The next day, it being calm, we hoisted out the boat to try whether there was a current, but found none.

On the 3rd, we took up more seaweed and another piece of wood covered with barnacles. The next day we saw two more seals, and a brown bird, about as big as a raven, with some white feathers under the wing. Mr. Gore told us that birds of this kind were seen in great numbers about the Falkland Islands, and our people gave them the name of Port Egmont hens.

On the 5th, we thought the water changed colour but, upon casting the lead, had no ground with 180 fathoms.

He writes in short, panting sentences, like a man too excited to string his words together.

On Friday, October the 6th, we saw land from the masthead, bearing W. by N., and stood directly for it: in the evening, it could just be discerned from the deck, and appeared large.

To the sharp eyes of a boy goes the credit of first sighting land, to him the gallon of rum and a kindly, immortal epitaph. "The South-West point of the bay I named YOUNG NICK'S HEAD, after Nicholas Young, the boy who first saw the land." At last, after the weary weeks at sea, something tangible. The next day it was calm and the ship nosed her way slowly inshore; excitement aboard was at fever pitch. "This land became the subject of much eager conversation; but the general opinion seemed to be that we had found the TERRA AUSTRALIS INCOGNITA."

A light breeze carried them gently towards a bay surrounded by white cliffs of a great height; behind, hills clothed in forest and trees of an immense size, hills, that gradually rose, towering one above the other and terminating in a chain of mountains which appeared to be far inland and of an enormous height.

> We also saw smoke ascending from different places on shore. We saw several canoes standing across the bay, which, in a little time, made to shore, without seeming to take the least notice of the ship; we also saw some houses, which appeared to be small, but neat; and near one of them a considerable number of the people collected together, who were sitting upon the beach, and who, we thought were the same that we had seen in the canoes. Upon a small peninsula, at the north-east head, we could plainly perceive a pretty high and regular paling, which enclosed the whole top of a hill: this was also the subject of much speculation, some supposing it to be a park of deer, others an enclosure for oxen and sheep. About four in the afternoon we anchored on the north-west side of the bay, before the entrance of a small river, in ten fathoms

water, with a fine sandy bottom, and at about a league from the shore.

Cook had discovered New Zealand, striking land near the middle of the east coast of the North Island. Six months of surveying were to produce charts of an unsurpassed brilliance; naturally they were only a rough outline of the coast, but a French naval officer who visited New Zealand two years later said this of Cook's charts, they were "of an exactitude and of a thoroughness of detail which astonished me beyond all powers of expression: I doubt whether our own coasts of France have been delineated with more precision."

That evening, Cook, Banks, Solander, and a party of men went ashore in the pinnace and yawl, landing on the east side of the river, and for the first time Europeans set foot on New Zealand. On the opposite bank they could see a group of natives whom Cook wished to speak to, and he ordered the yawl to carry them over, but at their approach the natives fled. However, they landed and walked up to some huts about two or three hundred yards from the waterside. Behind them in the bushes four pairs of eyes followed their every movement, four brown faces suffused with hatred and a savage fighting fury, their hands grasping deadly, fourteen-foot-long spears. The bushes parted and with the speed of panthers the savages rushed at the defenseless boys, sitting unsuspecting in the yawl. Just in time the coxswain of the pinnace saw them and yelled desperately to the boys to drop down stream; the boys instantly obeyed, still closely pursued by the natives. The coxswain fired a shot over their heads, momentarily checking them, but still they advanced, brandishing their spears in a most threatening manner; a second shot was fired over their heads without the slightest effect and as the leading savage steadied himself to hurl his lance at the boys, the coxwain fired a third time, killing the man in the very act of flinging his spear. The other three stood motionless for some minutes, as if petrified with astonishment, then fled, dragging after them the dead body, until their terror won and they dropped the corpse to hasten their flight.

On hearing the first shot Cook and his party drew together and hurried back to the boat; crossing the river they saw the native lying dead on the ground, shot through the heart. Examining the body they were astounded by its exact similarity to Abel Tasman's description, written a hundred and twenty-eight years previously; but here is Cook's description.

> He was a man of middle size and stature; his complexion was brown, but not very dark and one side of his face was tattooed in spiral lines of a very regular nature; he was covered with a fine cloth, of a manufacture altogether new to us, and it was tied on exactly according to the representation in Valentyn's Account of Abel Tasman's voyage.

Prudently they returned to the ship; all night they could hear the excited, noisy chatter of the natives on shore, probably discussing the awful terror that had come among them. The suddenness of that unprovoked attack puzzled and distressed Cook; sixty years later, however, a Mr. Polack discovered the reason.

In relating Cook's transactions in this bay, I must also mention the account given me by Manutai, grandson of Te Ratu, a principal chief, who headed the attack on the Englishmen, and was the first native killed by the Europeans. It appears that the tribes who now assaulted Cook had not been long in possession of the land, as they were originally a party of strangers from the southward who had made war on the inhabitants of this place, and had defeated and destroyed them. This decisive battle had taken place but a very few years previously to the arrival of Cook, and Te Ratu had been one of the principal warriors. Another chief was shot in the shoulder; this man recovered, and died within a few years previously to my visiting these localities in 1836. I saw the son of this wounded warrior, an elderly man, who pointed out to me, on his body, the spot where the ball had passed through the shoulders of his father. Cook's ship was at first taken for a bird by the natives; and many remarks passed among them as to the beauty and size of its wings [the sails]. But on seeing a smaller bird, unfledged, descending into the water and a number of parti-coloured beings, but apparently in the human shape, also descending, the bird was regarded as a houseful of divinities. Nothing could exceed the astonishment of the natives.

When their leader was killed,

the manner of his unseen death was ascribed to a thunderbolt from these new gods: and the noise made by the discharge was represented as thunder. To revenge themselves

> was the dearest wish of the tribe; but how to accomplish it with divinities who could kill them at a distance without even approaching to them was difficult to determine. Many of these natives observed that they felt themselves taken ill by only being particularly looked upon by these Atuas. It was therefore agreed that, as these new-comers could bewitch with a single look, that the sooner their society was dismissed the better it would be for the general welfare.

During *Endeavour's* stay the natives found little to better their first impressions of the English and indeed Cook, as will be seen later, was continually restraining his ship's company from committing atrocities. He alone stood out quite remarkably, for these are the words of the Maoris who had never before seen a white man: "The goblins lifted their walking sticks up and pointed them at the birds, and in a short time thunder was heard and a flash of lightning was seen, and a bird fell from the trees; and we children were terrified and fled away." And of Cook: "we knew that he was the Chief of the whole by his perfect gentlemanly and noble demeanour. He seldom spoke, but some of the goblins spoke much. He was a very good man and came to us children and patted our cheeks and gently touched our heads." They are astounding, extremely touching words. There was an amazing quality in Cook that immediately impressed itself on others, whether nobleman, rough seaman, or savage.

Above all else, Cook wanted to establish friendly relations with the Maoris; and with this foremost in his mind, landed the next morning in three boats manned with seamen, marines, the gentlemen, and Tupia. About fifty natives appeared to be waiting for their landing, on the opposite side of the river. Cook took this as a sign of fear, so to dispel their suspicions he stepped ashore accompanied only by Banks, Solander, and Tupia, and with his own particular brand of cool, calculating courage, advanced towards them; but before they had taken a dozen paces the Maoris were on their feet flourishing their weapons, evil-looking clubs which Cook described as being "well contrived for close fighting, as they would certainly split the thickest skull at a single blow," and long barbed lances which they handled "with such strength and agility that we can match them with no weapon but a loaded musquet." Tupia shouted in the language of Tahiti, but this seemed only to infuriate them more. Against this savage opposition Cook retreated till the marines could be landed, then again advanced with only three companions and Tupia, a very brave act. Tupia was directed to speak to them "and it was with great pleasure that we perceived he was perfectly understood, he and the natives speaking only different dialects of the same language."

This was the first sign of an extraordinary string of circumstances undeniably linking the Tahitans and Maoris, despite the distance between the two lands — in a straight line it is over two thousand miles.

Without the slightest difficulty, Tupia told the Maoris that all the English desired was water and provisions, frequently breaking off his conversation to turn uneasily to Cook and warn him "they are not our friends, they are not our friends." The success of the expedition, the health of the ship's company, depended on that vital necessity, fresh provisions. Tupia continued to urge them to trade and at last one of them stripped and swam over without his arms; almost immediately two more followed, and soon after twenty or thirty more, but all armed. As they approached, Tupia warned again and again, "They are not our friends, be upon your guard." The Maoris set little value on the offered presents of iron and beads, but showed great interest in the sailors' weapons, trying to give their own clubs in exchange, their tempers worsening at their failure. Tupia's warning soon proved true, for they attempted, unsuccessfully, to grab the weapons and Cook was obliged to warn them that any further attempts would result in death. But in vain, for one of the Maoris snatched a piece of equipment from Green and danced away, waving it insolently round his head, shouting with exultation. The action gave his companions courage. They increased their hostilities, and since Cook could see a further group advancing, it became absolutely necessary to take strong action. Banks fired, and hit the man with small shot, but although slightly wounded he continued to flourish his stolen trophy. This so infuriated Monkhouse that he fired and the native dropped, but without in the least deterring the advance of the other Maoris. In a situation so critical, Cook had no option but to fire a volley, which happily checked them and they retired upcountry.

Regretfully Cook realized that nothing was to be done with the people at this place, and finding the river water salty, he decided to look farther afield, hoping at the same time to induce or, if possible, "surprise some of the natives, and take them on board, where, by kind treatment and presents, I might obtain their friendship, and by this means establish an amicable correspondence with their countrymen."

A dangerous surf made it impossible to land elsewhere in the bay, but they saw two canoes to seaward and Cook decided this would be a favourable opportunity to take some of the natives, for they were probably fishermen without arms, and he had three boats, full of men. The boats were deployed so as to intercept the canoes in their passage to the shore; the first proved altogether too swift and easily evaded the English; the second canoe, too, seemed likely to outstrip them, so a musket was fired over their heads. At the shot they stopped paddling, and seeing them strip. Cook thought they were going to take to the water. He was mistaken, for with incredible savagery and an animal braveness they attacked the boats, using their paddles, stones, and any weapon they could lay their hands on. Taken completely off his guard, and in the heat of battle, Cook ordered his men to fire, an order that he regretted to the end of his days. Out of the seven natives in the canoe, four were instantly killed and the other three leapt into the water, swimming with tremendous speed and resisting capture with ferocious vigour. Eventually they were overpowered and taken into the boats, where they squatted down like rabbits too frightened to resist further, waiting to be killed. Presents were heaped on them and, incredulous, they realized they were to live. By the time they reached *Endeavour,* "they appeared to be not only reconciled to their situation, but in high spirits, and upon being offered some bread when they came on board, they devoured it with a voracious appetite."

Through Tupia they asked and answered many questions and, before lying down to sleep, ate another large meal. During the night, however, the awfulness of their situation struck them afresh, "they sighed often and loud." But the gentle Tupia comforted them, soothing away their fears with his soft Polynesian words; slowly their confidence returned and expressed itself in song. Aboard the little ship the men heard for the first time the sweet, melancholy sadness of Maori music; beautiful, haunting melodies that affected them deeply. "Solemn and slow, like those of our Psalms."

To James Cook, lying sleepless and harassed in his cabin, his mind at war between his duty and humanity, those songs tore at his sensitive brain. His regret at the killing of the four Maoris was an intense pain, for it might have been avoided. He got up, reached for quill and paper and wrote:

> I am conscious that the feeling of every reader of humanity will censure me for having fired upon these unhappy people, and it is impossible that, upon a calm review, I should approve it myself. They certainly did not deserve death for not choosing to confide in my promises: or not consenting to come on board my boat, even if they had apprehended no danger; but the nature of my service required me to obtain a knowledge of their country, which I could not otherwise effect than by forcing my way

> into it in a hostile manner, or gaining admission through the confidence and good will of the people. I had already tried the power of presents, without effect; and I was now prompted, by my desire to avoid further hostilities, to get some of them on board, as the only method left of convincing them that we intended them no harm, and had it in our power to contribute to their gratification and convenience. Thus far my intentions certainly were not criminal, and though in the contest, which I had not the least reason to expect, our victory might have been complete without so great an expense of life; yet in such a situation, when the command to fire has been given, no man can restrain its excess, or prescribe its effect.

Banks was equally depressed by the incident, deeply ashamed that, though they outnumbered the Maoris, yet they had resorted to the use of firearms; "black be the mark for it," he wrote, "and heaven send that such may never return to embitter future reflection."

Quite certainly, Banks was far the more honest of the two. "Upon a calm review," wrote Cook; if we analyze the incident, it is clear that the Captain was anything but calm at the time. The whole conception of the idea was clumsy, for from the brief contact he had had with the Maoris it was evident that they were fearless and fierce, certainly not likely to take kindly to being kidnapped. Thereafter, it was a matter of pure speculation that they would understand the giving of presents to be a kindness or act of friendship. And again, "in such a situation, when the command to fire has been given, no man can restrain its excess, or prescribe its effect." The effects of gunfire is beside the point. The mistake was in ever giving the order to fire. Two native canoes outmanoeuvred Cook, the Maoris bid fair to beat him in a standup fight, and the incident is so unlike Cook that one is forced to this conclusion. He completely lost his sense of judgement, and, more important still, he lost his temper.

In the morning the three Maori boys seemed cheerful, eating another enormous meal; then they dressed them with bracelets, anklets, and necklaces, Cook hoping that they would spread the news on shore of the kindness of the English. On indicating to the youths where he intended to land them, the happy expressions on their faces turned to stark horror, "because, they said, it was inhabited by their enemies, who would kill them and eat them." The killing was accepted as possible, but the eating was taken merely as a figure of speech. Nevertheless, Cook took no chances and put the boys ashore at a point they chose, not leaving them till they were safely in the custody of their friends.

IX

STAATEN LAND

October, 1769 – March, 1770

TO THE civilized world and the ship's company on *Endeavour,* New Zealand was still a mystery, the land Cook had found might prove to be the mighty southern continent. Certainly nothing was to be gained by staying longer at their present anchorage. "The next morning, at six o'clock, we weighed, and stood away from this unfortunate and inhospitable place, to which I gave the name of Poverty Bay."

Cook coasted northwards, keeping closer inshore than was perhaps prudent, amid appalling navigational dangers. A lesser man might have been content to stand well out to sea, just keeping the land in sight, merely satisfying himself as to its rough outline, whether it was an island or a continent. It is impossible to stress too strongly the firm courage needed to carry out this type of surveying. The dangers were there, clearly evident before his eyes; a mistake on his part would result in a certain, highly unpleasant death for every man aboard, for there was no second ship to rescue the survivors of a mistake on the Captain's part, or an act of God.

Cook's own description of the first near-disaster cannot be bettered, for he was not a man given to overstatement.

We kept turning out of the bay till the afternoon, and about ten o'clock we were suddenly becalmed, so that the ship would neither wear nor stay; and the tide or current setting strong, she drove towards land so fast that, before any measures could be taken for her security, she was within a cable's length of the breakers. We had thirteen fathoms water, but the ground was so foul that we did not dare to drop our anchor; the pinnace, therefore, was immediately hoisted out to take the ship in tow, and the men, sensible of their danger, exerting themselves to the utmost, and a faint breeze springing up off the land, we perceived with unspeakable joy that she made headway, after having been so near the shore that Tupia, who was not sensible of our hairsbreadth escape, was at this very time conversing with the people upon the beach, whose voices were distinctly heard, notwithstanding the roar of the breakers. We now thought all danger was over, but about an hour afterwards, just as the man in the chains had cried "seventeen fathoms" [eighty feet of water under the ship, certainly a strong enough reason to think themselves safe] the ship struck. The shock threw us all into the utmost confusion; Mr. Banks, who had undressed himself, and was stepping into bed, ran hastily up to the deck, and the man in the chains called out "five fathoms"; by this time the rock on which we had struck being to windward, the ship went off without having received the least damage, and the water very soon deepened to twenty fathoms.

It must be repeated: after such a narrow escape, Cook

would have been justified in keeping clear of the treacherous coast. He might well have reported to the Admiralty on his return the existence of New Zealand, but added a rider to the effect that the dangerous nature of the shoreline did not justify him hazarding one of His Majesty's ships, without a second vessel standing by in case of accident.

But those are idle speculations in the case of James Cook. During the charting of New Zealand he was twice more as near to shipwreck, the inevitable risks of navigating in completely unknown waters at the mercy of the wind, tide, and current. The second near-disaster occurred a few weeks later.

> At this time it was nearly calm, and the tide of ebb setting out, we were in a very short time carried by the rapidity of the stream close upon one of the islands, which was a rock rising almost perpendicularly out of the sea. We perceived our danger increase every moment, and had but one expedient to prevent our being dashed to pieces, the success of which a few minutes would determine. We were now within little more than a cable's length of the rock, and had more than seventy-five fathom of water.

Cook let go his anchor and by a hundred-to-one chance found a bottom that held. That in itself would not have saved them, but that day the hand of Providence was over the little ship, for more cable had been let go than the distance from where the anchor had dropped, to the island; but for the current's making a tiny alteration of course as it neared the land, their end would have been quick and decisive. Strung out on the end of their cable like a fish on a line, just over forty feet away from the jagged rocks, they waited and watched. "In this situation, we were not above two cables length from the rocks: and here we remained in the strength of the tide, from a little after seven till near midnight." Then wind and a change of current came to their rescue and they got away safely.

A third near-miss was over and done with before they knew of the danger they were in. They passed some rocks "on which the sea broke in a dreadful surf. As we passed these rocks to the north in the night, and discovered the others under our bow at break of day, it is manifest that our danger was imminent, and our escape critical in the highest degree; from the situation of these rocks, so well adapted to catch unwary strangers, I called them the Traps."

It may be thought that the danger of running aground has been overstressed; after all, they were near to the shore and it was probable they would be able to scramble to dry land and safety. In addition, the ship's company included skilled craftsmen, carpenters, shipwrights, blacksmiths, and Cook himself had worked in the dockyards during his merchant service apprenticeship. More than once before shipwrecked mariners with these advantages and salvaged timber from the wrecked vessel had built themselves a sufficiently serviceable vessel to reach safety.

Nevertheless, there was not a man aboard who, in the event of the ship's breaking up, would not have preferred to drown rather than be left to the mercy of the Maoris. For as *Endeavour* slowly circled the North Island those few words spoken by the Maori boys, "Do not put us ashore there, it is inhabited by our enemies who will kill and eat us," began to grow into a hideous reality. Yet, even as fresh evidence came to light that these people were indeed cannibals, the ship's company still refused to believe the truth their eyes told them. "Tupia inquired if it was their practise to eat men, to which they answered in the affirmative; but said that they ate only their enemies who were slain in battle." This was not taken too seriously, for the crew had been left in little doubt that they were regarded as enemies, and this was no more than bluff.

But a few days later, when they were trying to persuade some of the natives aboard, the gentlemen gasped in horror as the Tahitan priest quietly told them why the Maoris were not too keen to accept their invitation. "Tupia interpreted what they said, and we were much surprised to find that, among other arguments, they assured the people in the canoes, we did not eat men. We now began seriously to believe that this horrid custom prevailed amongst them; for what the boys had said we considered as a mere hyperbolical expression of their fear." Soon further concrete evidence was laid before them. "This day, some of our people found in the skirts of the wood, near a hole or oven, three human hip bones, which they brought on board: a further proof that these people eat human flesh."

Finally, amid the virgin beauty of the forest and the sweetness of the songs of innumerable birds — "their number was incredible, and they seemed to strain their throats in emulation of each other, this wild melody was infinitely superior to any that we had ever heard of the same kind: it seemed to be like small bells, most exquisitely tuned" —

they witnessed the horrible, gruesome sight of men gnawing human bones with rapacious and obvious relish, their faces and hands smeared with blood, and picking the remains of human gristle from their teeth.

> At this sight we were struck with horror, though it was only a confirmation of what we had heard many times since we arrived upon the coast. As we could have no doubt but the bones were human, neither could we have any doubt but that the flesh which covered them had been eaten. They were found in a provision-basket: the flesh that remained appeared manifestly to have been dressed by fire; and in the gristles at the end were the marks of the teeth which had gnawed them.

Cook, Banks, and Solander were scientists with instructions "to observe the genius, temper and disposition of the natives." Coldly, dispassionately, they continued their investigation into this frightful custom, producing what must be an almost unique, on-the-spot piece of journalism. Few men have witnessed cannibals eating human flesh and lived to tell the tale. This was but a small Maori family, not more than a dozen at most, yet "upon inquiry who the man was whose bones we had found, they told us that about five days before, a boat belonging to their enemies came into the bay, with many persons on board, and that this man was one of the seven whom they had killed." Nothing more than a few bones were left when Cook and his party came upon the family; their meat ration had been slightly over one human body a day.

Still they continued to investigate. Banks, holding a human arm, pretended to disbelieve their story, whereupon one of the cannibals "bit and gnawed the bone which Mr. Banks had taken, drawing it through his mouth, and showing by signs that the flesh to them was a dainty bit."

Tupia carried on the conversation,

> during which they repeated what they had told us already. "But," said Tupia, "where are the heads? Do you eat them too?" "Of the heads," said an old man, "we eat only the brains, and the next time I come I will bring some of them to convince you that what we have told you is truth." After some further conversation between these people and Tupia, they told him that they expected their enemies to come very shortly to revenge the death of the seven men whom they had killed and eaten.
>
> Our old man kept his promise and brought on board four of the heads of the seven people who had been so much the subject of our enquiries: the hair and flesh were entire, but we perceived that the brains had been extracted: the flesh was soft, but had by some method been preserved from putrefaction, for it had no disagreeable smell.

After a great deal of haggling, Banks finally persuaded them to sell him one of the heads, but they would part with no more.

After this, the old joke of the cannibal politely enquiring the name of his victim, in order that the menu might be correctly written up, failed to raise a laugh aboard the *Endeavour*.

With infinite patience, skill, and courage, Cook continued to coast round North Island anticlockwise, in weather that was frequently far from ideal for surveying. But his charts were superb, for he deplored inaccuracy: "the chart though perhaps not equally exact, is without any error of moment, except possibly in some few places, which are here, and in other parts of the chart, distinguished by a dotted line." A new conception for explorers. His predecessors in the Pacific would never have dreamed of a dotted line. They allowed themselves a glorious amount of artist's license, drawing in large continents as the mood took them.

Cook's method was simple and designed for maximum safety: the dangers were there and on occasions risks had to be deliberately taken, but as far as conditions allowed, the Captain surveyed fresh ground by day, returning to the safety of his own soundings by night. In this way he reached Tasman's "Cape Maria Van Diemen," receiving hints from the Maoris of another huge land to the northwest.

> We inquired farther, if they knew of any country besides their own: they answered that they had never visited any other, but that their ancestors had told them that to the Northwest there was a country of great extent.

Could it be possible that these splendid seamen, the Maoris, had indeed visited Australia? Tupia dismissed their story as nonsense, asking if they had "brought any hogs with them when they returned; they said, 'No.' 'Then,' replied Tupia, 'your story is certainly false, for it cannot be believed that men who came back from an expedition without hogs had ever visited a country where hogs were to be procured.' " Cook was inclined to believe them, he was interested by the fact that the Maoris referred to hogs by name, the same word as in Tahiti; no description was necessary despite the fact that in New Zealand they never saw a pig.

Link by link a fascinating chain was welding itself together, undeniably connecting the Society Islanders with the Maoris and even the South American Indians. The distances are vast. From Tahiti to the nearest point of New Zealand is over two thousand miles, or roughly the same as a line across the Atlantic Ocean from Ireland to Newfoundland. Yet if these people had drifted on rafts guided by currents, they would have covered twice that distance, for the current between the two lands sweeps in a great arc.

On one occasion, a "boy swam over to us, bringing in his hand a green branch, which we supposed, as well here as at Otaheite, to be an emblem of peace." There was the exact similarity of language; and remarkably, the same religion:

> . . . among other natives who came down to them was a priest, with whom Tupia entered into a very learned conversation. In their notions of religion they seemed to agree very well, which is not often the case between learned divines on our side of the ocean: Tupia, however, seemed to have the most knowledge, and he was listened to with great deference and attention by the others.

The women mourned for their dead in precisely the same way as the Tahitans, inflicting frightful wounds on themselves.

> She sat upon the ground near the rest, who, one only excepted, seemed not at all to regard her; the tears constantly trickled down her cheeks, and she repeated in a low, but mournful voice words which even Tupia did not at all understand. At the end of every sentence she cut her arms, her face, or her breast with a shell which she held in her hand, so that she was almost covered with blood, and was indeed one of the most affecting spectacles that can be conceived.

On one of their visits ashore "an old man showed us the instrument they use in the staining of their bodies, which exactly resembled those that were employed for the same purpose at Otaheite." They found a plant "of which these people, as well as those of Otaheite, make cloth." But here the connection went even farther east, for Cook noted that they "have two sorts of cloth, which have an even surface, and are very ingeniously made, in the same manner with that manufactured by the inhabitants of South America."

Finally, both Tupia and the Maori priests of New Zealand had the same confused traditionary notions of a great land to the northeast, from which they had a common belief their ancestors originated. Tahitans and Maoris both believed *Endeavour* was a fulfilment of an ancient folklore story, a visitation from their ancestors.

Cook recorded these similarities, but made little comment on their significance. He was more pleased at the convenience of a common language than surprised at the amazing coincidence. Perhaps with such a variety of fresh scenes and experiences he was past being amazed, for he and all the other gentlemen aboard lumped together the inhabitants of South America, the Society Islands, New Zealand, and Australia as Indians, without suggesting any difference of race. With the exception of Australia, they were probably very near the truth.

After rounding Cape Maria Van Diemen, Cook sailed south until he reached the huge opening, laid down by Tasman as a bay, although he did admit the possibility of its being a strait. It was named by Banks Cook's Strait, but the modesty of the great navigator shows clearly in his journal, for he makes no mention of the incident himself, apart from a chapter heading.

At this point Cook took possession of the land, taking a post

> to the highest part of the island, and after fixing it firmly in the ground, I hoisted upon it the Union flag, and honoured this inlet with the name of Queen Charlotte Sound: at the same time taking formal possession of this and the adjacent country, in the name and for the use of His Majesty King George the Third. We then drank a bottle of wine to her Majesty's health, and gave the bottle to the old man who had attended us up the hill, and who was mightily delighted with his present.

They remained for a month in the bay, careening the ship, Banks collecting specimens and the Captain working on his charts. One day during their stay Cook took a walk by himself to the top of the highest hill in the neighbourhood, and to his joy was able to see the eastern ocean; he was overlooking Cook's Strait. In his own mind he was now convinced he had discovered an island, but not so his officers, for there "was a notion which some of the officers started, that Eaheinomauwe [the Maori name for North Island] was not an island." They believed the land stretched away indefinitely to the southeast. To convince them Cook rounded the southern point of North Island, naming it, after his old friend, Cape Palliser, thence north to the point where they had first struck New Zealand. "I then called the Officers upon deck, and asked them whether they were not now satisfied that Eaheinomauwe was an island: they readily answered in the affirmative, and all doubts being now removed, we hauled our wind to the eastward."

The island had been circumnavigated but it had not been possible to explore any of the country inland, owing to the extreme hostility of the Maoris. Cook constantly tried to get on friendly relations with them, but with small success; they were a warlike, incredibly brave people, determined to rid themselves of the visitors. No opportunity was ever lost to trade with them, the Captain even buying useless rubbish, hoping that any sort of a start might lead to better relations. Whenever possible he persuaded them aboard, loading them with presents and kindness, but seldom achieving much.

Continually, without warning or provocation, *Endeavour* was attacked by great sinister war canoes, sixty-eight feet long, two-thirds the length of the ship, filled to capacity with warriors armed with their deadly lances, hurling stones at the ship and screaming out their war cries. "Come to us, come on shore and we will kill you all with our patoo-

patoos." Not one, but dozens of these canoes attacked at a time, flying towards the little ship with a graceful, dangerous swiftness.

> I have seen the strokes of fifteen paddles on a side of one of their canoes made with incredible quickness, and yet with such minute exactness of time that all the rowers seemed to be actuated by one common soul.

In self-defense Cook was forced to fire at them, spattering them with small shot. On occasions this checked them, but it was equally likely to infuriate these magnificently brave people. Even when wounded they would howl their defiance, breaking into war dances of a savage beauty, consisting of

> a great variety of violent motions, and hideous contortions of the limbs, during which the countenance also forms its part: the tongue is frequently thrust out to an incredible length, and the eyelids so forcibly drawn up that the white appears both above and below, as well as on each side of the iris, so as to form a circle round it: nor is anything neglected that can render the human shape frightful and deformed; at the same time they brandish their spears, shake their darts and cleave the air with their patoo-patoos. This horrid dance is always accompanied by a song; it is wild, indeed, but not disagreeable, and every strain ends in a loud and deep sigh, which they utter in concert. In the motions of the dance, however horrid, there is a strength, firmness and agility which we could not but

> behold with admiration; and in their songs they keep time with such exactness that I have often heard above a hundred paddles struck against the sides of their boats at once, so as to produce but a single sound.

On rare occasions they were persuaded to come alongside, but even then they had to be watched, for they were ready to snatch at anything within reach. One day they grabbed Tupia's boy servant, and made off with him, but luckily he was rescued from the cannibal's pot, paralyzed with terror. Cook named the bay where this incident occurred Kidnapper's Bay. They never knew whether they were being offered the hand of friendship or death:

> . . . naked and despicable as they were, they sang their song of defiance, and seemed to denounce against us inevitable destruction: they remained, however, some time out of stone's throw, and then venturing nearer, with less appearance of hostility, one of our men went to the ship's side, and was about to hand them a rope: this courtesy, however, they thought fit to return by throwing a lance at him, which having missed him, they immediately threw another.

By being constantly on the alert the ship's company avoided casualties: "their ammunition was not, indeed, dangerous to anything but the cabin windows." But no captain, past or present, appreciated his windows being smashed.

If everyone aboard had tried as hard as Cook to create

friendly relations with the natives things might have been better. Too often, when he was off the ship, his officers allowed themselves to be drawn into situations in which, to preserve their own face, they behaved with the typical brutality of their century. They cannot really be blamed, for they were the normal products of their age. Cook, with his philosophical understanding of primitive people, his patience and kindness, would be outstanding in any age.

The following extracts from Cook's journal indicate clearly the difficulties he constantly met with from his own officers. Leaving Mr. Gore, the Second Lieutenant, in charge of the ship, the Captain went ashore to stretch his legs. Alarmed by the firing of a gun he returned, only to learn that the second lieutenant considered himself grossly misused by one of the Maoris. Certainly he had been provoked, for he had agreed to buy a piece of native clothing,

> but the Indian, as soon as he had got Mr. Gore's cloth in his possession, refused to part with his own, and put off the canoe. Upon being threatened for this fraud, he and his companions began to sing their war-song in defiance, and shook their paddles: still, however, they began no attack, only defying Mr. Gore to take any remedy in his power, which so provoked him that he levelled a musket loaded with ball at the offender while he was holding the cloth in his hand, and shot him dead.

Pretty drastic action, and as Cook said: "It would have been happy if the effect of a few small shot had been tried upon this occasion, which, upon others, has been successful."

The stupidity of Mr. Hicks, the First Lieutenant, very nearly caused a nasty clash. Again Cook was out of the ship. Hicks discovered a native in the theft of a half-minute glass and "took it into his head to punish him by giving him twelve lashes with the cat-o'-nine-tails; and accordingly ordered him to be taken to the gangway, and tied up to the shrouds." His companions, incensed with rage, grabbed their weapons and streamed over the ship's side to rescue him. It was entirely due to the coolness of Tupia's reasoning that the natives were restrained from further violence. Hicks, however, remained inexorable and the punishment was inflicted:

> . . . as soon as the criminal was unbound an old man among the spectators who was supposed to be his father gave him a hearty beating and sent him down into his canoe. All the canoes then dropped astern and the people said that they were afraid to come any more near the ship — their cheerful confidence was at an end, and their stay short: they promised, indeed, at their departure, to return with some fish, but we saw no more of them.

One of the midshipmen who had been defrauded in a bargain had recourse, for revenge, to an expedient which was equally ludicrous and severe. He got a fishing line, and when the man who had cheated him was close under the ship's side in his canoe, he heaved the line with so good an aim that the hook caught him by the back. He then pulled the line, the man held back, and the hook broke in the shank, leaving the barb sticking in the flesh.

Cook descended with an iron fist on any of the ship's company who wronged the natives, reverting to the lash to impress upon them that if it was wrong for the Maoris to steal it was doubly evil in them.

> Some of our people, who, when the Indians were to be punished for a fraud, assumed the inexorable justice of a Lycurgus, thought fit to break into one of their plantations and dig up some potatoes: for this offence I ordered each of them to be punished with twelve lashes. After which two of them were discharged: but the third insisting that it was no crime in an Englishman to plunder an Indian plantation, though it was a crime in an Indian to defraud an Englishman of a nail, I ordered him back into his confinement, from which I would not release him till he had received six lashes more.

By degrees, they discovered that the warlike qualities of the Maoris were not confined to attacks on the ship; they were continually fighting savagely among themselves. High rail fences on the tops of hills, which they often saw, and at first supposed had some religious significance, turned out to be strongly fortified villages, well nigh impregnable and stocked with sufficient food to withstand months of siege. The Maoris were ever on the alert against each other. If for any reason they were away from their villages for a night they always slept in a circle, the women and children in the centre, the men on the outside, their hands grasping their weapons even in sleep. From a demonstration a warrior gave them of their fighting methods they were left in no doubt of the primeval savagery of their battles.

> A post or stake was set up as his enemy, to which he advanced with a furious aspect, brandishing his lance, which he grasped with great firmness; when [the post] was supposed to have been pierced by his lance, he ran at it with his patoo-patoo, and falling upon the upper end of it, which was to represent his adversary's head, he laid on with great vehemence, striking many blows, any one of which would probably have split the skull of an ox. From our champion's falling upon his mock enemy with the patoo-patoo, after he was supposed to have been pierced with the lance, our gentlemen inferred that in the battles of this country there is no quarter.

Fallen victims were, of course, eaten.

Cook considered that the basic reason for their continual, internal wars, and indeed cannibalism, was shortage of food. Unless a family could win for itself, and retain a pitch by the coast, enabling them to live on fish, they starved. It was his opinion that colonization of New Zealand by Europeans would be of as equal a benefit to the Maoris as to Great Britain.

With all their faults, the Captain considered them, as indeed they are, a splendid, brave people. They were scrupulously clean in their habits, which was more than enough to endear them to James Cook. So impressed was he with their cleanliness, that one evening he entertained his officers with a most amusing story on the subject. They nearly burst the buttons from their breeches in convulsions of laughter, and ashore, the Maoris crouching round their campfires wondered what strange nonsense had seized the horrid white goblins, as peals of laughter drifted across the water to them.

Here it is, for it would be inexcusable not to include it in any work connected with Cook. His salty wit is just as much a part of him as his magnificent, scientific brain:

> Every house, or every little cluster of three or four houses was furnished with a privy, so that the ground was everywhere clean. The offals of their food, and other litter were also piled up in regular dunghills, which probably they made use of at a proper time for manure.
>
> In this decent article of civil economy they were beforehand with one of the most considerable nations of Europe; for I am credibly informed that, till the year 1760 there was no such thing as a privy in Madrid, the metropolis of Spain, though it is plentifully supplied with water. Before that time it was the universal practise to throw the ordure out of the window during the night into the street, where numbers of men were employed to remove it, with shovels, from the upper parts of the city to the lower, where it lay till it was dry, and was then carried away in carts, and deposited without the gates. His present Catholic Majesty, having determined to free his capital from so gross a nuisance, ordered, by proclamation, that the proprietors of every house should build a privy, and that sinks, drains, and common sewers should be made at the public expense. The Spaniards, though long accustomed to an arbitrary government, resented this proclamation with great spirit, as an infringement of the common rights of mankind, and made a vigorous struggle against its being carried into execution. Every class devised objections against it, but the physicians bid the fairest to

> interest the king in the preservation of the ancient privilege of his people; for they remonstrated that if the filth was not, as usual, thrown into the streets, a fatal sickness would probably ensue, because the putrescent particles of the air, which such filth attracted, would then be imbibed by the human body. But this expedient, with every other that could be thought of, proved unsuccessful, and the popular discontent then ran so high, that it was very near producing an insurrection; his Holiness, however, at length prevailed and Madrid is now as clean as most of the considerable cities in Europe. But many of the citizens, probably upon the principles advanced by their physicians, that heaps of filth prevent deleterious particles of air from fixing upon neighbouring substances have, to keep their food wholesome, constructed their privies by the kitchen fire.

As at Tahiti, Cook allowed space in his journal for a description of the Maori girls. "The women were not impregnable," he writes with a nice gallantry, but was pleased to note a greater sense of modesty among them. For one day they surprised a group of girls groping for lobsters on the sea bed; they had removed their skirts to keep them dry.

> The chaste Diana, with her nymphs, could not have discovered more confusion and distress at the sight of Actaeon than these women expressed upon our approach. Some of them hid themselves among the rocks, and the rest crouched down in the sea till they made themselves a girdle and apron of such weeds as they could find; and

> when they came out, even with this veil, we could perceive that their modesty suffered much pain by our presence. [But, says Cook,] they were plain, and made themselves more so by painting their faces with red ochre and oil, which, being generally fresh and wet upon their cheeks and foreheads, was easily transferred to the noses of those who thought fit to salute them; and that they were not wholly adverse to such familiarity, the noses of several of our people strongly testified: they were, however, as great coquettes as any of the most fashionable ladies in Europe, and the young ones as skittish as an unbroken filly: each of them wore a petticoat, under which there was a girdle, made of the blades of grass highly perfumed, and to the girdle was fastened a small bunch of the leaves of some fragrant plant, which served their modesty as its inner-most veil.

Quite naturally, the sailors were willing to endure the inconvenience of a little red paint, for the pleasures that followed: "the transgressions of such of our people as were guilty of ravishing a kiss from these blooming beauties were most legibly written upon their faces."

The circumnavigation of New Zealand's South Island proceeded in much the same way as that of the North, taking just under three months; but this time Cook sailed round the island clockwise, arriving back at Queen Charlotte's Sound towards the end of March. They found the natives slightly darker in colour but of a similar disposition. Both men and women seemed to be mild and gentle: "they treat each other with the tenderest affection, but are implacable towards their enemies, to whom, as I have observed, they never give quarter." Those are kindly words, but Cook could understand that the Maoris supposed them to be their enemies, and attached no blame to it.

The ship's company's greatest blessing was the marvellous supply of fresh fish they enjoyed and the simplicity with which it could be caught, a few casts with the seine net producing 300 pounds. In addition they were able to salt away good stocks. It is interesting to note that individual messes were responsible for their own future supplies: "every mess in the ship, that was not careless and improvident, salted as much as lasted many weeks after they went to sea." Oysters there were in plenty, and it was nothing for the men to eat a boatload in a day, certain of a future supply on the morrow: "the oysters, which were as good as ever came from Colchester, and about the same size, were laid down under the booms, and the ship's company did nothing but eat them from the time they came on board till night, when, as may reasonably be supposed, a great part of them were expended."

Cook had sailed round both islands; he had completed his orders. The ship had finished her storing and was ready for the long run home. "I resolved to quit the country and return home by such a route as might be of most advantage to the service."

The Captain was greatly in favour of returning to England the way they had come, round South America. "I had myself a strong desire to return by Cape Horn." He had satisfied himself that between South America and New Zealand, above latitude 40° south, there was no "Terra Australis," but that, despite this, the world still continued to turn round — disappointing for the armchair theorist at home. He had totally disproved the "theoretical arguments which have been brought to prove that the existence of a southern continent is necessary to preserve an equilibrium between the two hemispheres; for upon this principle what we have already proved to be water would render the southern hemisphere too light."

He admitted there was still room to squeeze this vast, unknown land the Royal Society were so anxious and certain he would find into the limited amount of Pacific Ocean he and other explorers had missed, and that was his reason for wishing to return by the Cape Horn route. "This voyage has reduced the only possible site of a continent in the southern hemisphere, north of latitude 40°, to so small a space I think it would be a pity to leave that any longer unexamined."

But always keeping to the forefront of his mind the well-being of his ship's company, and knowing that such a return route was bound to be fraught with gruelling hardship, he called a conference of his officers and the gentlemen to discuss their future movements. In the cool dimness of the wardroom, Cook allowed himself to be persuaded that the danger of a return home by Cape Horn was courting disaster. Their voyage had achieved much and all the invaluable discoveries they had made would be lost to England should their brave little ship prove unequal to the task. The same was true of returning direct by the Cape of Good Hope. "It was, therefore, resolved that we should return by the East Indies, and that with this in view we should fall in with the East coast of New Holland."

It seems odd to think that while in England and Europe politicians, kings, statesmen, princes, and diplomats squabbled incessantly over a few square yards of land in the German states, a handful of brave young Englishmen, quietly discussing their future plans over a bottle of wine, came to a decision which added the great southern continent of Australia to the British Empire.

"At break of day on Saturday, the 31st March, 1770, we got under sail, and put to sea." Cape Farewell they named the cove they sailed from. Above Queen Charlotte's Sound, high in the hills, they had several times noticed and wondered at the existence of a lone wooden cross. The Maoris could give them no information; they said it had been there for generations, but they sometimes put flowers by it, as their fathers had done. "One monument, indeed, we observed of another kind—the cross that was set up near Queen Charlotte's Sound."

Were they, in truth, the first Europeans to set foot in New Zealand? Or had some earlier buccaneers strayed to the coast in years gone by? Perhaps that cross was the monument to the first real discovery of New Zealand. We shall never know.

They were on their way home. Abel Tasman's Staaten Land was now King George III's New Zealand. It faded from their sight. "Hurrah," shouted Banks, "a speedy return to England and roast beef."

X

TERRA AUSTRALIS

April–May, 1770

"On Saturday the 31st March, 1770, we steered westward with a fresh gale," sailing towards a land that was little more than legendary, for the only information Cook could gain from the charts he carried showed the southern tip of the island now known as Tasmania and a little of the western and northern coasts of Australia. The east coast which he hoped to strike and survey was an uncharted, unexplored blank. With only four months' provisions left, a ship that was in as good a condition as could be hoped, though that was far from perfect, a cheerful, brave ship's company, and most important of all, a healthy one, with confidence in their Captain, *Endeavour* again buffeted westward into the unknown.

In the absence of any other evidence, Cook thought it prudent to set course for Tasman's Land, because of "the longitude laid down by Tasman, whom we could not suppose to have erred much in so short a run as from this land to New Zealand." But still with an entirely open mind, for already he had disposed of vast continents, Mr. Dalrymple's passage "quite through the middle of the continent of America," frightful colossi, eight feet high, and enormous goblins. Doubtless the learned geographers of Europe were going to be disappointed at their theories being so summarily and certainly swept aside.

For a fortnight they plied to the westward without sight or evidence of land, then on the 16th of April they discovered the first indications of an approaching shore. "We saw an egg-bird and a ganut, and as these are birds that never go far from the land, we continued to sound all night, but had no ground with a 130 fathoms." Sufficient to excite the men and make them intensify their search with increased vigilance. They were generally sailing in dirty, squally weather, sinking in the valleys of a great swell, rising bravely to the summit of the waves, buffeted by "a hard gale from the southward and a great sea from the same quarter."

At five o'clock on the 17th, "a small land bird perched upon the rigging, but we had no ground with a 120 fathoms. . . . In the morning of the eighteenth, we saw two Port Egmont hens and Pintado bird, which are certain signs of approaching land, and, indeed, by our reckoning, we could not be far from it." (If Tasman was to be relied on.)

Then on 19th of April, at six o'clock in the morning, Lieutenant Hicks turned quietly to the Captain. "Land ahead, sir." With those three words, the great, rolling southern continent of Australia, the biggest land-mass in the South Pacific, was added to the British Empire. Point Hicks, Cook named their first landfall.

The strong westerly gales they had encountered had driven *Endeavour* north of her course, north of Tasmania, to the extreme southeastern corner of Australia. Looking to the north, the new continent streamed away as far as the eye could see; to the west land stretched into the misty distance.

No sign of Tasman's Island, and for that reason Cook dismissed it, and to his dying day no one really managed to convince the great explorer of the existence of Tasmania or the strait between it and Australia. That discovery was left to Dr. Bass and Captain Flinders, who, twenty-eight years later, in 1798, sailed through the strait, now known as the Bass Strait, in an open boat.

Cook never recorded anything unless he had actually seen it with his own eyes. Tasmania, or Van Diemen's Land as it was then called, might exist, "yet as I did not see it, and as I found this coast trend N.E. and S.W., or rather more to the eastward, I cannot determine whether it joins to Van Dieman's Land or not."

What were their first impressions of the new continent? Generally, that it gave "a very agreeable and promising aspect." Smoke, curling gently up from several different places, left them in no doubt that it was inhabited. Mr. Parkinson, the artist aboard *Endeavour,* was enchanted; "like a gentleman's park," he declared. Cook gives a fuller description:

> it appeared low and level; the sea shore was a white sand but the country within was green and woody, which has a very pleasing appearance; it is of a moderate height, diversified by hills and valleys, ridges and plains, interspersed with a few lawns of no great extent, but in general covered with wood; the ascent of the hills and ridges is gentle, and the summits are not high.

Cook sailed north along the eastern coast, pushing on as fast as weather conditions, tide, and the necessity of charting the new continent would allow, for they were on their way home, not over-well provisioned. Steering along the shore with a gentle breeze from the southwest, they were often near enough to "distinguish several of the natives upon the beach, who appeared to be of a black or very dark colour."

Cook may have been prompted by those glimpses of the natives and the frequent signs of smoke rising from the valleys to call his ship's company together and give them a few terse pieces of advice on how to deal with savages, realizing that, sooner or later, they would have to land and make contact with the natives. One fact only supports that assumption. When eventually they did land, the behaviour of both officers and men was so remarkably changed for the better, so much more restrained — no throwing of fish-hooks, or shooting to kill in cold blood — that with one single exception of brutish stupidity, the voyage up the complete length of Australia was unmarred by any unpleasant incident. True, they were dealing with a very different type of native: with aborigines, who were as far separated from the culture of the Maori-Polynesian as horses from men. Nevertheless, with all his kindness and humanity, Cook is credited with a quick, violent temper; not the sort of rage that suffuses a man's reason in a swirling red sheet, but an ice-cold anger, that left his brain clear and allowed him in a few biting words to cleave through lies, leaving the offender stripped of excuses, mentally quivering as his flesh would quiver on the rare occasion when Cook resorted to the lash. It is only supposition, but the Captain's patience may have been exhausted by the many stupid incidents that had occurred both in the Society Islands and New Zealand. The safety of the ship was always foremost in his mind, and though no mention is ever made in his journal of the possibility of *Endeavour* being overpowered by a really determined, co-ordinated attack by the Maoris (they could have mustered thousands of warriors, who, when roused by their hideous war dance, were too drunk in their fury to worry about the loss of their own lives), it would have been utterly foolish to have dismissed that possibility and equally foolish to do anything that might incite the natives to such an attempt. The truth of that was only too tragically borne out forty years after Cook visited New Zealand, by an extract from the journal of the Reverend Mr. J. W. Stack, one of the earliest missionaries to New Zealand. He was sent to Whangaroa, where, he says, "the crew of the ship *Boyd* were killed and eaten in December 1809."

With his customary, methodical care, Cook continued north along the beautiful eastern coast, a shore alternating between bold, rocky points and golden sandy beaches, past a lovely mountaintop of perfect and symmetrical proportions, which Cook named the Pigeon House; so astoundingly regular are its features, that it looks almost man-made. Occasionally they caught glimpses inland of high mountains, "which almost everywhere in this country, appear large and lofty." But there was no opportunity to get ashore, for a large hollow sea rolling in from the southeast saved them the necessity of even lowering a boat; they could see the risk would be too great.

An attempt might have been made at Jervis Bay, but a strong feeling of let's-get-on, let's-get-home was now underlying Cook's decisions. Although the bay promised "shelter from the North East winds; yet as the wind was with us, it was not in my power to look into it without beating up [tacking against the wind, a slow business], which would have cost me more time than I was willing to spare."

Two days later, when about a couple of miles from the shore, an attempt was made to land. They could see natives walking on the beach, carrying a canoe, which led them to hope they were coming off to the ship, but they were disappointed. Cook therefore determined to land himself and hoisted out the pinnace and yawl; however, indicative of their sad state of repair, "the pinnace proved to be so leaky that I was obliged to haul her in again." Accompanied by Banks, Solander, Tupia, and four rowers, they pulled for that part of the shore where natives were squatting down on the rocks, apparently waiting for them. When the boat was within a quarter of a mile, they ran away into the woods. Much as the English would have liked to land, they found it impossible, for a great surf beat on every part of the beach and their little boat would have been smashed to pieces. They were forced to content themselves by gazing at the country and hoping for the reappearance of the native population, the aborigines.

> After many a wishful look, we were obliged to return, with our curiosity rather excited than satisfied, and about five in the evening got on board the ship. About this time it fell calm, and our situation was by no means agreeable. We were now not more than a mile and a half from the shore, and within some breakers, which lay to the Southward; but happily a light breeze came off the land, and carried us out of danger.

A constant and ever present threat. Against a strong inshore wind, they were practically helpless, for there was very little they could do to prevent themselves from drifting onto the rocks.

With that same breeze they continued northward and at daybreak discovered a large bay, which looked to Cook as likely a place as they had yet passed in which to land. Accordingly, the Master was sent ahead in the pinnace, now repaired, to sound and make a preliminary survey. Looking through their glasses they could see ten natives gathered round a fire, but immediately the pinnace approached they retired inland. When the Master returned, he made no excuses for not landing, for however great his curiosity might have been, the sight of the natives, "armed with long pikes and a wooden weapon shaped somewhat like a cimiter, using many threatening gestures and brandishing their weapons," was quite sufficient to discourage him. Added to which, the general appearance of the aborigines was not exactly welcoming. By most accepted standards, they are not a handsome people, and with their faces, breasts, and thighs painted in thick white and red stripes they must have made a terrifying first impression.

The "cimiters" later turned out to be boomerangs, which the aborigines use with an uncanny accuracy. The bay the Master had surveyed was first called Stingray Harbour, because of the great number of poisonous fish they saw. Later, after Banks landed and found himself in a veritable botanist's paradise, Cook humoured him by renaming the place Botany Bay.

Cook edged *Endeavour* slowly into the bay and early in

the afternoon anchored under the south shore, about two miles inside the entrance. As they came in they could see a few huts and several of the natives — men, women, and children — apparently fishing with long spears.

Now a sailing ship is a fine, brave sight none can resist, however used they might be to seeing them: there is something about a ship that irresistibly draws the eye. Wherever *Endeavour* had been, she had always attracted the attention of the natives, generally awing them; and though only a small vessel, she was huge compared to their own canoes, with her towering masts and intricate cobweb of ropes and rigging, her great spread of white canvas, glinting almost silver in the strong tropical sunshine. Yet, the aborigines, who it is certain had never in their lives seen such a sight — nor could their ancestors ever have looked on so strange a vessel and passed the story on — took no more notice of *Endeavour's* entrance into the bay then they would a passing gull. They neither pointed in amazement at her nor paused for a moment in their fishing. They were so "intent upon what they were doing, that although the ship passed within a quarter of a mile, they scarcely turned their eyes towards her."

There was something eerie about these strange, black people, hideously decorated, completely unmoved by the appearance of *Endeavour,* something primeval that sent a slight shudder of horror through the ship's company. This time they had arrived in a different world, which they did not quite understand.

The place where the ship anchored was abreast a small village consisting of about six or eight houses. While they were preparing to hoist out the boats they watched, fascinated, as an old woman, followed by three children, came out of the wood, all naked as the day they were born, "the old woman herself being destitute even of a fig leaf." She and the children were loaded with firewood and were met at the crude huts by three more younger children; occasionally they glanced at the ship "but expressed neither fear nor surprise." In a short time she kindled a fire and the four canoes came in from fishing. The men landed, hauled up the canoes and began to cook their food, still "to all appearances, wholly unconcerned about us, though we were within half a mile of them."

In this strange atmosphere of unreality, an uncomfortable sensation of being wholly ignored left them wondering if they really existed. However, the boats were lowered, manned, and set out from the ship with Tupia as interpreter. They hoped to land where they saw the most people, for since they had paid so little attention to the arrival of the ship in the bay it was expected they would be equally uninterested in an actual landing. As on other occasions, the aborigines bolted for the woods, with the exception of two men armed with lances about ten feet long, who advanced down the beach to oppose the invasion.

> They called to us in a very loud tone, and in a harsh dissonant language, of which neither we nor Tupia understood a single word. They brandished their weapons and seemed resolved to defend their coast to the uttermost, though they were but two, and we were forty. I could not but admire their courage, and being very unwilling that

> hostilities should commence with such inequality of force between us, I ordered the boat to lie upon her oars.

True enough, Cook's whole mental make-up rebelled against taking unfair advantage, but there was more to it than that. He was not often at a loss, but this time he was completely baffled. How could he, or anyone else in the boats, guess that the few yards separating them from the aborigines did, in fact, cover millions of years of the history of the world? For the first time modern man was face to face with prehistoric Stone Age man, defending with animal courage the flight to safety of his female mates and their young, and instinctively resenting any intrusion into the oblivion of their age-old solitude. Cook called it courage, and if we can call the brave fluttering of partridges courage, desperately distracting the attention of an enemy while the young chicks scamper to safety, then he had chosen the right word.

Unable to understand a word of the native's harsh chatter, the Captain endeavoured for a quarter of an hour to demonstrate by signs that they bore nothing but goodwill and a desire to obtain fresh water. A few nails, beads and other trifles were thrown. The natives picked them up and seemed pleased, waving encouragingly to the boats. The moment they pulled for the shore they were again opposed. One now appeared to be a youth about nineteen or twenty, and the other a middle-aged man. Reluctantly the Captain ordered a musket to be fired between them, which seemed momentarily to scare the younger of the two, who dropped his bundle of lances, but immediately snatched them up again and, as if further to impress the invaders of his staunchness, hurled a stone at them.

A second musket loaded with small shot was fired and struck the eldest about the legs. Without uttering a sound, he turned and ran in the direction of the huts. It looked as if the brief engagement was at an end, so without further ado Cook beckoned to his nephew, Isaac Smith. "You go first, Isaac," said the Captain, and to the youngest member of the boat's crew went the privilege of being the first European to set foot on eastern Australia.

Eagerly the others jumped ashore, "but we had scarcely left the boat when the native returned, and we then perceived that he had left the rock only to fetch a shield or target for his defence. As soon as he came up he threw a lance at us and his comrade another. They fell where we stood thickest, but happily hurt nobody." A third charge of small shot was fired and with a final defiant gesture the natives hurled another lance, then ran for the woods.

Cook was anxious to follow, but deferred to Banks's better judgement when he suggested the lances might be poisoned, and contented himself with inspecting the huts. Inside one they found the children curled up like young rabbits, hiding themselves behind a shield. "We peeped at them, but left them in their retreat, without their knowing that they had been discovered." They left behind some beads, pieces of cloth, ribbons, and other presents, hoping they might procure the goodwill of the inhabitants, and took a bundle of lances, evil-looking weapons from six to fifteen feet long, pointed and barbed with fishbones as sharp as a razor, and smeared with a green viscous substance, which further confirmed Banks's theory that they might be poisoned.

Unable to find fresh water, they returned to the boats, passing on their way some of the native canoes. "We found them the worst we had ever seen." This was also their impression of the natives, echoing the words written some years previously by Dampier, who had seen the aborigines in northern Australia and had written of them:

> The inhabitants of this country are the miserablest people in the World. The Hodmadods, though a nasty People, yet for Wealth are Gentlemen to these. Their eyelids are always half closed to keep the Flies out of their Eyes they being so troublesome here that no Fanning will keep them from coming on ones Face and without the assistance of both Hands to keep them off, they will creep into ones Nostrils and Mouth too, if the Lips are not shut very close. They have great Bottle Noses, pretty full Lips and wide Mouths. They are long visaged, and of a very unpleasing Aspect.

Cook unwillingly endorsed that description, adding that they were "little advanced beyond mere animal life." As will be seen, every word he wrote about the aborigines was seasoned with a deep pity for these almost helpless people. Perhaps, with the deep understanding he had of his own age and its shortcomings, he could envisage the cruelty with which the natives were to be treated when Australia was eventually colonized. Quite unable to fend for themselves, and without the wit to escape from the first settlers, the aborigines were hunted down, flogged, killed, and tortured with a ruthless savagery that curdles the blood. "And Tupia himself, with an air of superiority and compassion, shook his head, and said that they were Taata Enos, 'poor wretches.' "

The next morning they went ashore again and this time were fortunate enough to find a fresh-water stream, sufficient for their wants. Lieutenant Hicks headed the watering party and during the afternoon was confronted with about eighteen aborigines, all armed, who advanced boldly to within a hundred yards of the English before halting. Hicks, however, acted with a decent restraint hitherto only exhibited by Cook, earning his praise. He "advanced to meet them, holding out presents to them as he approached, and expressing kindness and amity by every sign he could think of, but all without effect," for again they ran for the woods.

The Captain, with another party, went a second time to look at the native huts, and found them deserted. Even the few presents they had left the previous night were untouched and unmoved, lying exactly where they had been tossed down. "We were greatly mortified," said Cook. He left more valuable presents this time.

On the credit side they had found fresh water, oysters, "the largest I had ever seen," and an abundance of fish, for "in three or four hauls of the seine we took above three hundredweight of fish." But still, walking among the trees, which abounded with birds of exquisite beauty, loriquets, and cockatoos, flying in brilliantly coloured flocks, they felt the strange, eerie atmosphere of being in a completely different world. They discovered several small fires with mussels broiling on them, but not a trace of the natives was to be seen — just the uncomfortable feeling that they were being continually watched.

"We saw many houses of the inhabitants and places where

they slept upon the grass without shelter, but we saw only one of the people, who the moment he discovered us, ran away." They found the dung of animals, which they thought might be deer, clawed footprints like a dog's "and seemed to be about as big as a wolf." Banks's greyhound "which was with us got sight of it, and would probably have caught it, but the moment he set off he lamed himself against a stump which lay concealed in the long grass."

Sometimes they could hear the hushed chatter of the aborigines, or detect the whispering rustle of grass, but only occasionally could catch a brief glimpse of the natives as they fled deeper into the forest. They seemed an odd mixture of extreme timidity and, very rarely, great courage. The few contacts that the English made with them were indeed frightening affairs.

A midshipman accidentally strayed from the main party and suddenly found himself confronted by a very old man, a woman, and some little children. They were sitting under a tree by the waterside, and neither party saw the other till they were close together. Although the natives showed signs of fear they did not attempt to run away; the midshipman, too, was badly frightened but had sense enough not to bolt. He had nothing to give them except a parrot he had shot. They refused to accept it, shrinking back from his hand, either through fear or aversion. Seeing several canoes near the beach fishing and because of being alone, with the possibility of an attack, the man withdrew as quickly and with as much dignity as he could muster.

The ship's surgeon missed death by the merest fraction. Strolling near the watering place, he also strayed from his companions, and coming out of a thicket found his path barred by six natives about fifty yards ahead. One of them gave a loud shout. Instantly a lance was thrown at the surgeon from a different direction, "which very narrowly missed him." They immediately fled, another native slid down from a tree with the speed of a monkey and made off after the others as fast as his legs would carry him, leaving the officer in no doubt that the shout had been the signal for the throwing of the lance.

Quite certainly Mr. Gore underwent the most terrifying experience of their stay. It was followed by an act of stupidity by Monkhouse and by the coolest demonstration of bravery Cook exhibited in the whole of his adventurous life.

The Second Lieutenant had been sent out in the morning with a boat to dredge for oysters at the head of the bay. When he had collected a sufficient number he went ashore, taking a midshipman with him, and sent the boat away, intending to walk across country, join the watering party, and return with them to the ship. After a short time he had the feeling that he was being followed, and glancing quickly behind found a party of about two dozen natives, armed with their lances, not more than twenty yards from them. The moment he swung round and faced them they stopped. Still facing them, Gore and the midshipman took a step back, the natives took a step forward. It was obviously quite impossible to walk backwards the whole distance, besides, it would indicate fear to the aborigines. Mr. Gore marched on, the back of his neck tingling, and though he could not hear a sound from behind (the natives moved with the lithe silence of cats), he knew that nineteen yards from the small of his back were twenty savages, twenty poisoned lances. The suspense was appalling, the desire to run almost irresistible and quite impossible not to look behind. "He stopped and faced about, upon which they stopped also, and when he went on again, continued their pursuit." Many times Gore turned round and on each occasion the aborigines also stopped, their faces expressionless, only waiting for the Second Lieutenant to move again, then padding noiselessly behind. It was like a grim, deadly version of a child's game of mimic.

With sickening relief Gore caught sight of the watering party and with equal relief noticed the natives dropping farther behind, until by the time he rejoined his comrades, they had halted at about a quarter of a mile's distance.

Monkhouse, the surgeon, perhaps a little unnerved by his experience the day before, when, alone in the forest, a lance had been hurled at him, and perhaps overtopped with Dutch courage in front of the others, took it into his head to march on the natives, accompanied by three others. Boldly they set forth, full of the superiority of the white man, "but seeing the natives keep their ground till they came pretty near them they were seized with a sudden fear and made a hasty retreat." This was the kind of action, senseless, cowardly, and utterly stupid, that roused their quick-tempered Captain to a blazing fury. He used only ten words to burst Monkhouse's bravado, words that must have seared like a burn. "A sudden fear, very common to the rash and foolhardy."

The surgeon's action against a primitive people ensured the danger that it was hoped to avoid. Encouraged, four of the natives dashed forward and threw their lances at the fugitives, with such force that they flew forty yards beyond the retreating English, then howling derisively ran back into the woods.

That evening the aborigines returned again, screaming their defiance, and Cook could see that the situation was getting rapidly out of control, with the natives imagining they held the upper hand. He was essentially a man of action rather than words. His easiest line would have been to make them realize the death-dealing qualities of firearms, but it need hardly be emphasized that that was utterly repugnant to his nature. He knew as much about the aborigines as the reader now knows from what has been written. He was forced to admit they were little removed from animals; there had been many examples to show that in a body they were always willing to attempt to annihilate lone strangers. They were armed in one hand with a fearful lance — "it was indeed a most terrible weapon," writes Cook, and the English believed the sharp barbed points to be poisonous — and in the other hand with what was thought to be a scimitar, "which," said the sergeant of marines, "shone like a musket."

Yet, against fifteen savages armed like that, retreating into the woods, shouting their war cries, and with the knowledge that four of his own sailors had fled unchallenged from them, there was only one course open to a man of Cook's humanitarian nature and iron discipline. He sets it down so simply and briefly in his journal that it is easy to skim over it without realizing the calm bravery of the man who wrote it. "I followed them myself, alone and unarmed, for a considerable way along the shore, but I could not prevail upon them to stop."

Undoubtedly, the Captain took an unjustifiable risk in following the natives alone and unarmed, for it is true to say that his chances of returning alive from such a stroll along the shore were no more than fifty-fifty. But to Cook the issue was crystal clear. He had first to demonstrate to the aborigines that the invasion of their country was not warlike, and to his own ship's company that bravado, backed up by cowardice, was the worst possible way of dealing with an ignorant, savage people. His action was as cool as that of a surgeon performing an operation which might cause death but if left undone would certainly cause death, for James Cook believed implicitly in the rightness of his own methods and was willing to risk his life to prove them. It was a brave act, but if the immense amount of invaluable discoveries and material the expedition had gained is taken into account, must be judged almost as stupid as Monkhouse's. He was the Captain, his the responsibility of getting *Endeavour* safely home with her cargo of discoveries. A quiet word to Banks would have been quite sufficient for that immensely tough young man to demonstrate Cook's ideals to the ship's company. It is not easy to risk a friend's life, but in following the natives Cook not only endangered his own life, but that of every man aboard; for it is doubtful, extremely doubtful, if any other officer in the ship was sufficiently experienced to get *Endeavour* back to England. And Cook knew it.

Their stay at Botany Bay was nearly over; they had taken aboard everything fresh, by way of water and fish, they could find. The scientists had had a glorious time and the Captain had "caused the English colours to be displayed on shore every day, and the ship's name and the date of the year to be inscribed upon one of the trees near the watering places." They had done their best to assess the aborigines. "All the inhabitants that we saw were stark naked, they did not appear to be numerous, nor to live in societies, but like other animals were scattered about along the coast and in the woods." Farmer Cook had also taken careful note of the country "which I thought very fit for the production of grain of any kind."

"At daybreak on Sunday the 6th of May, we set sail from Botany Bay."

XI

SAILCLOTH AND SHEEP'S DUNG

May–June, 1770

About nine miles north of Botany Bay, they found themselves "abreast a bay or harbour in which there appeared to be a good anchorage, and which I called Port Jackson." Cook was in too much of a hurry to stop and so missed seeing Sydney, the finest natural harbour in the world, for he never returned to the eastern coast of Australia.

It was eighteen years later, in 1788, that the great modern port of Sydney was first founded, and its inception, though a digression from the story, is interesting, for the capital of New South Wales owes its origin to three curious circumstances: Cook's inaccurate assessment of Botany Bay, the over-fertile imagination of Banks, and Midshipman Matra, a particularly brutal member of the ship's company, though a typical product of the eighteenth century.

Why Cook gave such a glowing report of Botany Bay as a possible corn-growing district has always remained a mystery, for he was undoubtedly a pretty shrewd judge of land. So far as Botany Bay is concerned, he was wrong. At this time, too, Banks did not share Cook's enthusiasm for the bay. "Reading his journal," says Professor Woods, "we got the impression that he thought Botany Bay to be a very good place for botanists, but a very bad place for colonists." Fifteen years later, after the death of Cook, this same Matra wrote a report, suggesting that Botany Bay would be an ideal place in which to settle American loyalists, and Banks supported him, though he had previously made a verbal suggestion that the bay would be suitable as a penal settlement. His first impressions were considerably modified by this time, and perhaps, on glancing through his own journal and comparing it with Cook's, he may have thought to himself, "Well, after all, Cook was a farmer's son, born and bred, his assessment is likely to be more practical than mine," altering his earlier views for that reason.

Be that as it may, Banks's suggestion, not Matra's (or Magra as he sometimes called himself), was adopted. The first fleet of eleven ships, commanded by Captain Arthur Phillips and carrying seven hundred and fifty prisoners, arrived at Botany Bay on the 20th of January, 1788, after a voyage of eight months and one week. It took Phillips only a few days to decide that Captain Cook and Mr. Banks had been grossly inaccurate in the picture they gave of the bay, for he liked neither the water nor the land. Consequently, he sailed nine miles north to the next opening in the coastline and founded the modern city of Sydney — a city that has grown with incredible speed, making it difficult to compare the present fine streets and beautifully laid out parks with the sort of place it was as a convict settlement over a hundred years ago.

Of all the ship's company Midshipman Matra, judging by his behaviour on the voyage, is the last person one would imagine to have a serious thought in his head or to start writing reports on the best use to be made of eastern Australia, for he is the midshipman who did his utmost to persuade the other snotties to forsake the rigours of His Majesty's navy for the more comfortable existence of life with the exquisitely beautiful women of Tahiti.

The following, which occurred while cruising up the Australian coast, concerns poor old Mr. Orton, the ink-stained clerk, a man who only concerned himself with two sorts of liquid — ink and alcohol. It was far kinder to say of him that he had been seen drunk than that he had been seen sober; for his time was divided between quenching his enormous thirst and sinking into a blissful alcoholic slumber, from which even Lieutenant Zachary Hicks, with a voice like the last trumpet, could not rouse him.

Midshipman Matra, finding Richard Orton stretched out, happily insensible to the immense discoveries going on around him, conceived the brilliant idea of cutting off all his clothes as he lay sleeping. Whipping out his knife he stripped the old man naked and stood back to admire his handiwork. It did not satisfy him, however, and with a barbaric sense of humour, not untypical of his century, he again drew his knife and deftly sliced the lobes of both poor old Dick's ears as well.

His huge enjoyment of the joke was short-lived; the heavy hand of the Captain descended on his shoulder and sent him spinning to the quarter-deck, from which he was banished to the forward end of the ship for three weeks.

Cook never thought much of Matra, and the ear-cutting episode confirmed his opinion. In the seclusion of his cabin the Captain, still very angry, grasped his quill — "he being one of those gentry frequently found on board King's ships that can very well be spared," he wrote; "to speak more plainly, good for nothing," he added, then cooling down a little he scratched out the last sentence.

Some of Cook's written criticisms of his ship's company do sometimes seem rather strong. They were justified at the time and quite in place entered in the ship's log, but it was a little severe to include them in his own journal, which, modest though he was, he must have known would in all probability be published on their return home. For he could have had no doubts on the importance of the voyage or the wide interest his discoveries would be bound to arouse in England. Already, the first and second lieutenants had come in for some rough criticism and Monkhouse, the surgeon, was committed to paper as a coward for the part he played at Botany Bay when he ran away from the aborigines. Certainly Cook's criticisms were amply justified, but by including them in his journal, the indiscretions of his officers (and they were no more than that to the eighteenth-century mind) became public property, instead of a purely routine matter of discipline.

Endeavour continued to push northwards as fast as ever possible, keeping as close inshore as the Captain dared and taking advantage of all the wind they could get; even sailing at night if there happened to be a strong moon. They frequently saw smoke rising from the shore and on occasions caught glimpses of the natives, who never once evinced the slightest interest in the ship.

> Not one of them was observed to stop and look towards us, but they trudged along, to all appearances without

> the least emotion, either of curiosity or surprise, though it is impossible they should not have seen the ship by a casual glance as they walked along the shore; though she must, with respect to every other object they had yet seen, have been as stupendous and unaccountable to them, as a floating mountain with all its woods would have been to us.

Luckily they little knew of the fantastically dangerous waters they were approaching, but as they travelled north, naming the hills and the bays as they passed them, an indication of the appalling danger ahead was built up. "Mount Warning," and a little later, "Point Danger."

A landing was made at an inlet they named Bustard Bay because they shot one of the birds: "it was as large as a turkey and weighed seventeen pounds and a half. We all agreed that this was the best bird we had eaten since we left England; and in honour of it we called this inlet Bustard Bay."

They were now inside the Great Barrier Reef and navigation was becoming daily more difficult. Cook therefore decided to stop for a short time, replenish his water supply, wait for a better moon, and, if possible, lay the ship ashore to clean her bottom.

Accordingly the Captain and Master landed, accompanied by the usual party of scientists. "We soon met with several places where the ship might conveniently be laid ashore; but to our great disappointment we could find no fresh water." Because of this deficiency Cook named the inlet "Thirsty Sound," at the same time determining to make his stay as short as possible and only remain long enough to allow the botanists to collect samples.

They spent the day wandering among the beautiful blue gum trees, festooned with huge ant nests "made of clay, as big as a bushel." There were traces of the aborigines, too, nests of grass they had made for themselves "where four or five people appeared to have slept." And everywhere the air was thick with butterflies. "We found an incredible number of them so that for the space of three or four acres the air was so crowded with them, that millions were to be seen in every direction, at the same time every branch and twig was covered with others that were not upon the wing."

It is interesting to note that some years later Mr. George Bennet in his *Wandering in New South Wales* gives a particular description of these brilliantly coloured flocks of insects and their connection with the aborigines. It appears that the natives placed a high value on the butterflies as a luscious and fattening food, for their bodies contain a great quantity of oil. The collecting of the butterflies during November, December, and January was looked upon as a great festival. Smothering smoky fires were lit to suffocate the insects; they were then collected by the bushelful and roasted on prepared ground until their wings and down were singed off, and winnowed to separate the dust from the bodies. "They are then eaten or pounded by a piece of wood into masses or cakes resembling lumps of fat and may be compared in colour and consistency to dough made from smutty wheat mixed with a yellowish oily fat and resembling in taste a sweet nut." It sounds a nauseating mixture and the result of eating it very much as expected. "The first time this diet is used by the native tribes, violent vomiting and debilitating effects are produced; but after a few days they become accustomed to its use and then thrive and fatten exceedingly upon it."

Joseph Banks, irrepressible as ever, strode off into the bush with a few seamen, determined to penetrate more deeply into the country than anyone else. Soon they found their course obstructed by a swamp. Their terrible experience in the muddy waters of Tierra del Fuego makes it surprising that Banks contemplated attempting to cross. Quite undaunted, he plunged in, followed by the sailors, only to find themselves knee-deep in a black, stinking quagmire, and by the time they got halfway across, everyone, except of course Banks, was sorry they ever started, for "the bottom was covered with branches of trees interwoven with each other, sometimes they kept their footing upon them, sometimes their feet slipped through, and sometimes they were so entangled among them, that they were forced to free themselves by groping in the mud and slime with their hands." The swamp was about a quarter of a mile wide but they crossed right over, reaching the other side, plastered from head to foot in filth. They were rewarded with absolutely nothing except the sight of a few remains of food left by the natives as the English approached. They saw no one, so back through the mud they came.

Gore and a midshipman were treated similarly: "they said they had heard voices of the Indians near them, but had seen none."

Very briefly Cook summed up Thirsty Sound: "As I had not therefore a single inducement to stay longer in this place I weighed anchor at six o'clock in the morning of Thursday the 31st of May and put out to sea."

Cook was the first explorer of the eastern coast of Australia, but perhaps if he could have glanced at a chart of the coast and seen the nightmarish dangers that lay ahead, he might have been tempted to turn back. Running parallel to the coast is the formidable Great Barrier Reef, a reef that draws gradually tighter into the coast the farther north it goes, like a deadly pincer, forcing ships nearer to the pitiless rocks of the mainland—a jagged coral wall of destruction, inexorably squeezing in on the little Yorkshire coal boat. Every mile northwards narrowed the strip of water between the reef and the mainland, every day the space in which to manoeuvre shrank.

Looking north and east, the sea was studded with innumerable tiny islands, each one certain destruction, with the huge Pacific swell crashing the might of thousands of miles of unbroken ocean against them, spuming up into a glittering, silver spray, coldly beautiful, but as deadly as exploding gunpowder. Yet for every reef that could be seen, there were ten submerged, rising sheer from the ocean bed to within a few feet of the surface.

To navigate in those completely unknown waters called for a constant vigilance on which their lives depended. A boat was always kept ahead, passing back soundings to the Captain, but so irregular were the reports, jumping from twenty fathoms to two, that they never knew from one moment to the next which way they would have to steer.

It was fantastically dangerous, like a man hanging by his hands above a thousand upturned swords, knowing that sooner or later he must drop and certain that unless the million-to-one chance comes off, he could not hope to fall between the points, but must impale himself on them. This was the situation that faced Cook, and to stick to it calmly without once allowing signs of strain or worry to show on his face needed vast reserves of physical and mental toughness few men possess.

Nor had the Captain any idea how many miles of this gruelling navigation lay ahead. Tomorrow might see the end of it, or they might still be floundering around in the maze three months hence. He possessed only two scrappy pieces of evidence on the coastline ahead, neither of which could be much relied on. The first was from Quiros, the optimistic, cranky explorer who refused to give his helmsman a course because the Almighty would look after them. He was supposed to have sighted the islands they were now passing, "and which," as Cook cuttingly remarked, "some geographers, for what reason I know not, have thought fit to join to this land." The second hint was from the highly unreliable Dalrymple, for in the secret chart he had given Banks just before they sailed, there was shown a strait between northern Australia and New Guinea.

Whatever Cook's personal feelings about Dalrymple might have been, searching anxiously for a break in the coast to the northwest and a release from the dangers they found themselves in, he must have hoped desperately that his information was correct. Every mile of the shore was hopefully scanned, but there was no "indication of a passage to the North West." Ahead of them as far as the eye could see loomed danger, with a strong possibility of shipwreck and death. Even the iron will of the Captain was appalled at their future prospects and shows itself in his writing.

> Hitherto we had safely navigated this dangerous coast where the sea in all parts conceals shoals that suddenly project from the shore, and rocks that rise abruptly like a pyramid from the bottom, for an extent of two-and-twenty degrees of latitude, more than one thousand, three hundred miles; and therefore hitherto none of the names which distinguish the several parts of the country that we saw, are memorials of distress; but here we became acquainted with misfortune, and we therefore called the point which we had just seen farthest to the northward "Cape Tribulation."

From the choice of that sad name it seems almost as though James Cook could foresee dangers ahead of them that were nearly insurmountable. He had faith in his own ability as a seaman; his ship's company trusted implicitly to his skill; but he was wise enough not to deceive himself that even the combined brains of the finest mariners alive would probably be unequal to the task of getting his little ship through the tangled mass of islands that lay ahead.

As the hard glare of sunlight softened into the evening dusk, Cook took his ship farther out to sea, not wishing to attempt the dangers ahead until he had a clear day before him. From six o'clock to nine he gently edged *Endeavour* away from the land, pacing the deck in clear moonlight, with a fine, light breeze blowing from the west that exactly suited his purpose; and with a satisfying regularity, the soundings deepened gradually from fourteen to twenty-one fathoms and remained steady.

At nine o'clock, feeling happier about the situation than

National Maritime Museum, London

Captain James Cook, Fellow of the Royal Society. *Engraved by J. Basire from a painting by William Hodges.*

The frozen wastes of Christmas Sound, Tierra del Fuego. Here two of the ship's company perished. Another ten miraculously

National Maritime Museum, London

survived the icy blasts of this inhospitable land. *Engraved by W. Watts from a painting by William Hodges.*

The Island of Otaheite (Tahiti) bearing southeast distant one

National Maritime Museum, London

league. *Engraved by W. Watts from a painting by William Hodges.*

The fleet of Otaheite assembled at Opáree. The painter seems to have been thinking in terms of the grandeurs of classical an-

National Maritime Museum, London

tiquity. *Engraved by W. Woollett from a painting by William Hodges.*

Captain Cook, looking strangely like Washington crossing the Delaware, is welcomed by the natives of a friendly Pacific isle in

National Maritime Museum, London

an 18th-century interpretation. *Engraved by J. K. Sherwin from a painting by William Hodges.*

Another landing on a less friendly island. "Signs and threats having no effect, our own safety became the only consideration;

National Maritime Museum, London

and yet I was unwilling to fire on the multitude." *Engraved by J. K. Sherwin from a painting by William Hodges.*

A Maori in Cook's time. Most of them were heavily tattooed about the face. *Engraved by Michel from a painting by William Hodges, ca. 1772.*

National Maritime Museum, London

National Maritime Museum, London

South Sea Island woman from New Caledonia. *Engraved by Hall after a painting by William Hodges, ca. 1773.*

he had for some time, the Captain went below to snatch a quick supper, but he had scarcely seated himself before he was summoned frantically on deck again. Within the space of minutes the sea bed had suddenly shoaled from twenty-one fathoms to twelve, ten, and eight, or, when Cook jumped up hastily from his supper, there was a hundred and twenty-six feet of water beneath the ship and by the time he reached the upper deck only forty-eight feet. "I immediately ordered everybody to their station," and all was made ready to turn the ship back into deeper water and drop anchor to stop her, while the ground ahead was investigated by one of the boats. "But meeting at the next cast of the lead with deeper water again, we concluded that we had gone over the tail of the shoals which we had seen at sunset, and that all danger was past." Long before ten o'clock they were back to deep, steady sounding, drawing farther from the land into safer water. "The gentlemen left the deck in great tranquility, and went to bed!"

But again a few minutes before eleven, the water shallowed from twenty to seventeen fathoms, and within the seconds it took to swing the lead, *Endeavour,* with a shuddering, jarring shock struck the reef, grinding herself to a standstill on the knife-sharp coral.

In a few moments everyone was on deck "with countenances which sufficiently expressed the horrors of our situation." The ship remained immovable, except for the merciless heaving of the swell that beat her against the crags of rock on which she lay. "We had too much reason to conclude that we were upon a rock of coral, which is more fatal than any other, because the points of it are sharp, and every part of the surface so rough, as to grind away whatever is rubbed against it, even with the gentlest motions."

Immediately Cook ordered all the sails to be taken in and the boats hoisted out to examine the depth of water around the ship. They soon found that their position was even worse than they had at first feared, for the vessel had been lifted over a ledge of rock and lay in a hollow basin of coral, the edges of which, in some places, were no more than three feet below the surface. *Endeavour* was well and truly aground, ironically enough in the exact latitude in which Bougainville had approached the coast two years previously.

Every man aboard knew just how perilous was their situation. Scarcely beneath the horrified expressions of their faces lay a mad, murderous panic, for seamen of those days, highly superstitious as they were, obeyed only two laws in the face of imminent shipwreck and death. They refused to learn to swim, because it was only a means of prolonging the agonies of drowning, and they immediately broke into the wine and spirit stores, to get as drunk as possible in the short time left them to live.

But the calm efficiency of the Captain, reflected in his officers, checked their fears and kept the panic under control. With cool steadiness Cook gave his orders, anticipating dangers and keeping a couple of moves ahead, putting into operation the long tried and practical manoeuvres carried out under such conditions. The longboat was already out, sounding round the ship to discover where the deepest water lay, and the anchor was carried to that point, then, provided the anchor held, the capstan was turned in the hopes that the ship would wind herself towards the anchor, pulling her off the reef at the same time. But though the men pushed against the stubborn capstan spars till their hearts were fit to burst and the sweat poured off them, they could not budge her. They worked under terrible conditions, with the ship beating so violently against the rocks that they could hardly keep their feet. It seemed impossible that anything made by man could long withstand such a terrible battering; she must break up, and to complete the scene of distress they could see, by the light of the moon, great chunks of the vessel floating away around them; first the protective sheathing boards, specially added before they left England to protect the real ship's bottom, then with a sickening wrench the false keel broke away and drifted off "so that every moment was making way for the sea to rush in which was to swallow us up."

Their only chance was in lightening the ship, but they had missed the best opportunity, for she had struck right at high tide and as stores were thrown overboard the water also shallowed. Indirectly it helped. She settled more firmly on the coral and was not beaten against it with such violence. Their great hope lay in the next high tide, "but it was doubtful whether she could hold together so long, especially as the rock kept grating her bottom under the starboard bow with such force as to be heard in the fore store-room." Cook well knew it was an equal danger his men might break under the mental strain. "This, however, was no time to indulge in conjecture, nor was any effort remitted in despair of success." That strong attitude of determination, coupled with Cook's superb qualities as a leader, inspired his men. The gentlemen, too, acted with typical English phlegm. Green continued to take observation as though nothing had happened. Banks quietly lent a hand wherever necessary, nevertheless admitting that the Captain's firm handling of the situation impressed him more than anything on the voyage, for he speaks of "the cool and steady conduct of the officers, who, during the whole time, never gave an order which did not show them to be perfectly composed and unmoved by the circumstances however dreadful they might appear."

Immediate action was taken in preparation for the next high tide; the pumps were started in the hold, for they were leaking badly and everything that could be spared was jettisoned:

> . . . six of our guns, being all we had upon the deck, our iron and stone ballast, casks, hoop staves, oil jars, decayed stores and many other items that lay in the way of heavier materials, were thrown overboard with the utmost expedition, everyone exerting himself with an alacrity almost approaching to cheerfulness, without the least repining or discontent, yet the men were so far impressed with a sense of their situation that not an oath was heard among them.

They laboured unceasingly through the night to the accompaniment of the groans of a dying ship. As day broke, they could see land about twenty-five miles away, without any island between them and the shore, precluding the possibility, if *Endeavour* should go to pieces, of scrambling to safety while the boats ferried them to the mainland. With immense relief, however, they realized the wind was gradually dying away and early in the forenoon it was dead calm. If it had blown hard the ship must inevitably have been destroyed.

The next high tide was expected at eleven o'clock and the men waited tensely for the supreme effort they would have to make. Nearly fifty tons of equipment had been thrown overboard, but as the tide started to rise the water began to pour into the ship, for while they had rested securely on the bottom, the leak had not been too bad, but now it rushed in so fast that two pumps, worked incessantly, could scarcely keep pace with it.

Long before it was time, the sailors were waiting by the capstan; no orders were necessary, they longed for the word "go." Then at a signal from the Captain they threw themselves against the spars, pushing till their muscles throbbed, ached, and went numb with the strain and their heads lolled stupidly between their arms. But *Endeavour* still stuck fast, immovable as a mountain — "to our inexpressible surprise and concern, she did not float."

Cook did not allow his men to think about this second failure for an instant, but put them to work immediately, preparing for the next high tide. He now realized himself that the midday flood fell some feet short of the night tide and cheered his men on with the information. They worked on numbly, taking out two more anchors, hoping that by shortening the length of cable between the three anchors and the ship they might draw her off the ledge on which she rested towards deeper water. But they still had hours to wait before the attempt could be made.

By two o'clock in the afternoon, *Endeavour* was heeling giddily over to starboard, swaying drunkenly on the coral rocks. At five in the evening the tide began to rise. At the same time the leak increased so alarmingly that two more pumps were brought into action, but only one would work. Three pumps were kept going, and by a prodigious effort they managed to keep level with the inrushing water. By nine the ship was on an even keel, but the leak was gaining on them. It was only the terrific strength of the Captain's character that kept the men going, for fear gripped icily at their hearts. And that was the real victory: the unshakable respect of the ship's company for Cook was stronger than their combined fears.

But they were all aware of the real danger, for with the leak steadily gaining on them, it was more than likely that if *Endeavour* could be freed she would lose the support of the rocks she lay on and almost certainly sink.

> This was a dreadful circumstance, so that we anticipated the floating of the ship not as an earnest of deliverance, but as an event that would probably precipitate our destruction. We well knew that our boats were not capable of carrying us all on shore, and that when the dreadful crisis should arrive, as all command and subordination would be at an end, a contest for preference would probably ensue, that would increase even the horrors of shipwreck, and terminate in the destruction of us all by the hands of each other; yet we knew that if any should be left on board to perish in the waves, they would probably suffer less upon the whole than those who

should get on shore, without any lasting or effectual defence against the natives, in a country where even nets and fire-arms would scarcely furnish them with food; and where, if they should find the means of subsistence, they must be condemned to languish out the remainder of life in a desolate wilderness, without the possession, or even hope, of any domestic comfort, and cut off from all commerce with mankind, except the naked savages who prowled the desert, and who perhaps were some of the most rude and uncivilized upon the earth.

In fact, no other ship visited that part of the coast for the rest of the century. Nevertheless, to anyone who has had the slightest connection with the sea in more recent years, it sounds strange to hear Cook declare that the break-up of his ship would end his authority. It would be unlikely to happen today. Seamen of those days were kept under by a rigid, cruel discipline, without any of the flexibility of the modern navy. True, Cook was years ahead of his time in the treatment of his ship's company. But the crisis of death would erase his considerate treatment from the minds of his men, leaving an officer a pig, the Captain that had wrecked them the symbol of a crushing servitude. The harder the independent spring of man's nature is pressed down, the more violently will it react when released.

In that dreadful state of suspense they waited for death. The long day dragged by and the crucial moment that was to determine their fate drew near. They could read in each other's faces the horrible fears that were in their own minds.

By about twenty past ten that night, the tide had risen

sufficiently to float the ship, and as many hands as could be spared from the pumps were sent to man the capstan and windlasses. They knew that if they failed this time *Endeavour* would certainly not survive another twenty-four hours of the cruel battering she had taken. But with the last desperate effort, "she was heaved into deeper water." For a tense, immeasurable moment the level of water in the hold was watched, the seconds that were to decide their fate. Miraculously the leak did not increase; there was still a shred of hope, still life. The men, "having now endured excessive fatigue of body and agitation of mind for more than four-and-twenty hours, and having but little hope of succeeding at last, began to flag." None of them could stand the back-breaking toil at the pumps for more than five or six minutes at a time. Then, totally exhausted and quivering with fatigue, their breath coming in harsh, wheezing gasps, they flung themselves on the deck, though a stream of water was running over it from the pumps. A few moments of respite, till their mates threw themselves down and the others jumped to fight the inrushing sea, relieving each other until an accident very nearly tipped the scales from hope to despair.

The planking which lines the inside of a ship's bottom is known as the ceiling and between this and the outside planking there is a space of about eighteen inches. The man who had been taking the depth of water in the hold had done so to the inside planking, but on being relieved the next seaman took the depth to the bottom planking, so that within the space of a few minutes it appeared to the weary men at the pumps that the leak had gained eighteen inches. Exhausted to near breaking point, even the bravest were on the point of giving up the unequal struggle and in a few moments everything would have been in a state of complete confusion. This accident, however dreadful its consequences might have been, was soon righted, and instead of the murderous panic which the Captain knew only too well would be likely to follow, the men were imbued with a sudden joy that acted like a charm, inspiring fresh vigour:

> . . . they renewed their efforts with such alacrity and spirit, that before eight o'clock in the morning the leak was so far from having gained upon the pumps, that the pumps had gained upon the leak. Everybody now talked of getting the ship into harbour as a thing not to be doubted.

By eleven o'clock, with a fair breeze from seaward, they got under sail and stood towards the land.

It was, however, quite impossible to sustain very much longer the terrific effort that had been made at the pumps. They had been at it ceaselessly for nearly thirty-six hours and their faces were lined and drawn with fatigue. In this situation one of the midshipmen made a suggestion — quite new to Cook — which eventually saved them. He took a piece of sail and stitched lightly to it handfuls of chopped-up wool and oakum, smearing sheep-dung and other filth on it. The sail thus prepared was hauled under the ship's bottom by ropes which kept it extended, and when it came under the leak, the suction which carried in the water sucked in the sail, effectively bunging up the hole. "By the success of this expedient our leak was so reduced, that instead of gaining on three pumps, it was easily kept under with one." (Just how successful that ingenious method for stopping leaks has proved, is interesting. H.M. ships now always carry mats, ready made up for such an emergency, known as collision mats. They look rather like a huge featherbed mattress and have been in constant use right up to and through the Second World War. Those mats have certainly, over the last hundred and seventy years, saved many tens of lives. However, the speed of modern sea warfare makes the operation — fothering as it is called — too slow and ships travel so much faster nowadays that the mats are apt to be dragged off.)

There are two more points of interest about the midshipman's mat: it was smeared with sheep's dung. So there were still live sheep aboard *Endeavour* embarked in England two and a half years previously, for no mention is made of any being taken on board during the voyage; in fact they had only touched at two places where live sheep might have been purchased — Madeira and Rio de Janeiro — and Cook makes no mention of any such purchase at either port, though all other bought stores were carefully noted down in his journal. It can therefore be assumed that they were original livestock from England.

That the sheep were alive, or had been to within a couple of days before striking the reef, is absolutely certain. Cook would not tolerate unnecessary filth in any ship he commanded throughout his life: in fact his ships were reported to reek of vinegar, used as a detergent.

Nor was the mat the midshipman's own idea; he had, in fact, seen it used by the master of a merchantman, who had such faith in it that he sailed his ship right across the Atlantic from Virginia to London, though he could have had the leak properly repaired before leaving Virginia. Such a feat must undeniably have left a strong impression on the midshipman's mind, yet, so strong was the iron curtain around commanding officers of those days, Cook included, that *Endeavour's* leak was perilously near to beating them before the young officer dared to make a suggestion to his Captain.

Like a faithful, old, wounded dog, *Endeavour* started to limp over the painful twenty-five miles between her and the shore. A brave little ship kept afloat by a few square feet of canvas and sheep's dung: humble enough articles to save the southern Pacific from plunging back into its age-old obscurity. A bit of sailcloth preserving for Britain the secrets and ultimate possession of the mighty continent of Australia and the rich lands of New Zealand.

XII

ENDEAVOUR RIVER

June–August, 1770

VERY GENTLY Cook edged his ship to within two miles of the shore, sending ahead a couple of boats to hunt for a suitable bay, for it was absolutely essential to beach *Endeavour* as soon as possible.

The first bay investigated proved too shallow, but at nine o'clock that night the pinnace returned with the news that they had found an ideal harbour with fresh water and a high enough rise and fall of tide to allow the ship to be put ashore. They weighed anchor at six o'clock the next morning, keeping two boats ahead as an essential precaution, but despite every possible care they only just missed running aground again, skimming over the top of a reef with barely four feet of water between the ship's bottom and the rocks.

They were in a better position than when lying on the rocks, but still in great danger, for the ship was not working well, answering the helm with sluggish indifference. The wind was freshening to gale force and they were entangled among the shoals onto which Cook feared they might be driven before his boats could mark the channel entrance to the bay. To speed up the operation the Captain went personally in the pinnace to buoy the entrance, but by the time he had finished the weather had so far worsened that an attempt to get inside the harbour that night would have been suicidal. There was nothing for it but to anchor and let the gale blow itself out.

Every conceivable precaution was taken for their safety, "for in all the joy of our unexpected deliverance, we had not forgot that at this time there was nothing but a lock of wool between us and destruction."

For two days they lay strung out on the end of their cable, unable to move, silently wondering at the strange freak of the weather that had preserved them while they lay hopelessly floundering twenty-five miles out to sea on the reef. It blew hard before they grounded; it blew hard for the rest of their stay on the coast. "It was calm only when we were upon the rock, except once; and even the gale that afterwards wafted us to the shore, would then certainly have beaten us to pieces."

Cook desperately wanted to get his ship safely into the harbour, for troubles were heaping themselves on him.

> The scurvy now began to make its appearance among us, with many formidable symptoms. Our poor Indian Tupia, who had sometimes before complained that his gums were sore and swelled, and who had taken plentifully of our lemon juice by the surgeon's directions, had now livid spots upon his legs, and other indubitable testimonies that the disease had made a rapid progress, notwithstanding all our remedies. . . . Mr. Green, our astronomer, was also declining; and these, among other circumstances, embittered the delay which prevented our going on shore.

On the morning of the seventeenth, though the wind

was still blowing hard and only the absolute necessity of getting into the bay prompted Cook, he ventured to weigh anchor and push into the harbour. Twice during the attempt they ran aground, their nerves strained to breaking point. The first time they slid off easily, but the second time stuck fast and only freed themselves by making a raft of some of the masts alongside the ship; this, with a rising tide, saved them, and by evening they were safely moored alongside the steep beach of the little bay. "It is remarkable, that in the whole course of our voyage we had seen no place which, in our present circumstances, could have afforded us the same relief." Small wonder he wrote those words; any safe anchorage was a paradise after the gruelling battle they had fought.

First thoughts were for the sick — now nine seamen, Green, extremely ill, and Tupia. Get them ashore and get some fresh food into them was the essential thing. A tent was set up for them, but provisions of fresh food, even fish, seemed scarce. Tupia instinctively knew what his body needed, he "employed himself in angling, and lived entirely upon what he caught, recovering in a surprising degree."

When everything possible had been done for the sick members of the crew, Cook turned his attention to the wounds of his ship. From the amount of water admitted the Captain knew she must be badly hurt, as he himself was, for the grinding scrunch of her bottom on the rocks had seemed to him as if his own flesh were being ripped with a coarse file. Nor would Cook be the only man aboard similarly hurt; for to any seaman worth his salt an intangible friendship grows up between man and ship; inexplicable, seldom if ever mentioned, but nevertheless strongly there, and generally the farther away from the distractions of home, the greater the affection and respect.

As the Captain prepared to beach *Endeavour,* his own recommendation for her choice must have run through his mind with pleasing strength.

> She must also be of a construction that will bear to take the ground, and of a size which, in case of necessity, may be safely and conveniently laid on shore, to repair any accidental damage or defect. These properties are not to be found . . . in any other but North country ships such as are built for the coal trade. . . .

The forge was landed, the blacksmith and armourer set to work making nails, bound to be needed in the repair; and to the merry chink of hammer on anvil, the ship's company set to work clearing stores from the forward end, where the leak was, to the beach, and moving some to the stern, so as to rear up the bows of the ship and drop the stern. Thus, bows up, stern down, assuming the position of a motorboat at high speed. At the apex of a high tide, *Endeavour* was pulled on to the steep beach. It took several days to prepare the ship for this manoeuvre, which sounds simple, but in fact required a nice sense of judgement and balance from Cook. The sequence is simple to follow; *Endeavour's* bows were poised much farther over dry beach than they would have been if she had remained on an even keel, and as the tide receded her bows settled gently down on dry land, with her stern still floating. The tide finally left them at two o'clock in the morning, revealing to their horrified eyes the extent of the damage.

As they gazed in numb silence at her injuries they realized, fully now for the first time, how hairbreadth had been their escape, how relentlessly the sharp, jagged coral had sawed into the ship: "there was not a splinter to be seen, but all was smooth as if the whole had been cut away by an instrument." Yet their preservation had finally depended on the most extraordinary, million-to-one chance. Cook, and many others aboard, had fully expected *Endeavour* to go to the bottom once she lost the support of the rocks, and so she would have done had not a piece of coral broken off and remained sticking in the planking as the ship slid off the reef: "one of the holes, which was big enough to have sunk us, if we had had eight pumps instead of four, and been able to keep them incessantly going, was in a great measure plugged up by a fragment of the rock, which, after having made the wound, was left sticking in it." Round this lump of coral, bits of the midshipman's "collision mat" had jammed themselves, more or less stopping the worst of their leaks. The rest of the damage was to the protective sheathing and false keel, which they had seen drift away in the moonlight as they lay helpless on the rocks taking that dreadful beating. What was left "was in so shattered a condition that it had better have been gone."

Suddenly Banks, who had also been inspecting the damage, scrambled aboard and rushed to the stern of the ship. His specimens, his precious specimens gathered with such painful care, were in danger, for he had moved the whole of his curious collection of plants to the bread room in the after end of *Endeavour,* and now "the position of the ship was very near depriving the world of all the knowledge which Mr. Banks had endured so much labour to procure."

There they all were: bottles, butterflies, pressed plants, potted plants, birds' feathers, shells, and drawings, bobbing about in the now almost flooded compartment, a lot of them under water. However, by indefatigable care and attention, most of them were restored to a state of preservation, but some were entirely spoiled and destroyed.

It was to take them six weeks to restore *Endeavour* to seaworthiness; six weeks during which their main attention was directed to living off the land, for it was essential to preserve the small remaining stock of feeding stuffs. They had assured themselves of a supply of fresh water before beaching *Endeavour,* but their first efforts to procure fresh food were disappointing, nearly catastrophic, for the lives of those suffering from scurvy were wholly dependent on fresh food. At certain times of the day they could see the water of the bay broken up into shimmering ripples as shoals of fish rose to feed, twisting their sleek silver bodies in quick, glinting curves as they snapped at the flies, hovering low over the water. But though the men cast the seine net again and again they returned at night with only three fish at most. Then slowly their luck changed; from three the number jumped to twenty, sufficient to give the sick a reasonable feed. They found a type of plant which made quite good greens, and finally Cook was pleased to enter in his journal: "I was able to distribute two pounds and a half of fish to each man: the greens that had been gathered I ordered to be boiled among the pease, and they made an excellent mess, which, with two copious supplies of fish, afforded us unspeakable refreshment." Variety was added to their diet by cockles, the biggest they had ever seen, and delicious fresh turtles, weighing about two hundred and sixty pounds apiece. Once they shot a land animal, an utterly strange, weird creature, unlike anything they had ever seen or heard of before: "its progress is by successive leaps or hops, of a great length, in an erect posture." Inevitably, contact with land animals meant contact with the aborigines, in this part of the coast as in others — timid, furtive creatures, almost animal. Seldom seen, but often sensed and heard, darting swiftly out of sight at the approach of the English. They did manage, however, to extract from the natives a name for the strange, hopping animals. "Kanguroo," Cook called it (an amusing mistake that has endured to the present day). Years later, if only we had been fortunate enough, we should have seen learned naturalists and dignified naval officers in frock coats hopping about the beach of Endeavour River, before an astonished crowd of aborigines. "The word 'kangaroo' was repeatedly used to them last year, accompanied by an imitation of the leap of the animal, which the natives readily understood." But after each splendid series of exhausting hops and the word "kangaroo," the natives sadly shook their heads. "Men-u-ah," they repeated again and again. A fairly accurate translation from Cook's word "kanguroo" is, "I don't know," or, "I don't understand you." Still, it stuck and to this day the animal remains a "kangaroo," an "I-don't-know."

Give it what name you like, the important thing to Cook and his men was that it ate well.

> The next day our kanguroo was dressed for dinner, and proved most excellent meat; we might indeed be

> said to fare sumptuously every day; for we had turtle in great plenty, and we all agreed that they were much better than any we had tasted in England, which we imputed to their being eaten fresh from the sea, before their natural fat had been wasted, or their juices changed by a diet and situation so different from what the sea affords them as garbage and a tub.

By far the greater part of the sailors' time was taken up hunting or fishing. Frequently they slept out at night. We can picture them, after a hard day's marching, throwing themselves to the ground, tired out, drowsily discussing round the campfire the strange sights they had seen that day.

> Their beds were plantain leaves, which they spread upon the sand, and which were as soft as a mattress; their cloaks served them for bed clothes, and some bunches of grass for pillows. . . . Here then they lay down, and, such is the force of habit, they resigned themselves to sleep, without once reflecting upon the possibility and danger of being found by the natives in that situation.

That may sound strange, but familiarity undoubtedly breeds contempt. These men had been through every conceivable danger, witnessed human flesh eaten, seen animals stranger than the unicorns of their childhood fairy stories, and brushed shoulders with a type of man scarcely removed from beasts. No wonder that they had grown a little blasé. One of the midshipmen, an American, was certain he had seen a wolf, exactly like those of his own country; to which Cook added, "there are wolves upon this part of the coast, if we were not deceived by the tracks upon the ground." Here they were mistaken, it was probably a dingo. They found a large nest built with sticks twenty-six feet in circumference and two and a half feet high, which they were utterly unable to account for. They investigated great ant heaps, "but though we gratified our curiosity at their expense, the injury did not go unrevenged; for thousands immediately threw themselves upon us and gave us intolerable pain with their stings."

They sampled every type of coconut they could find and in consequence gave themselves terrible diarrhea: "they operated as an emetic of great violence." Still not satisfied, but sufficiently interested to test the strength of the aborigine's stomach against a pig's, as well as their own,

> judging that the constitution of the hogs might be as strong as the natives, though our own had proved to be so much inferior, we carried them to the sty: the hogs ate them, indeed, and for some time, we thought, without suffering any inconvenience; but in about a week they were so much disordered, that two of them died, and the rest were recovered with great difficulty.

So Farmer Cook put an immediate stop to any further experimental comparisons of stomach strength, however fascinating that branch of research might be.

Wonder grew on wonder, culminating in one of the seamen rushing back to the ship trembling from head to foot and as white as a sheet. He had seen the devil with two horns and as black as old Nick.

> . . . we naturally inquired in what form he had appeared, and his answer was in so singular a style that I shall set it down in his own words: "He was," says John, "as large as a one gallon keg, and very like it; he had horns and wings, yet he crept so slowly through the grass, that if I had not been afeared, I might have touched him."

Wisely, the seamen refrained from challenging him. Probably he was too badly frightened to get a word out. Banks later identified this formidable apparition as a flying fox, an extremely ugly bat only found in the East and Australia.

Through all these adventures, Cook was most anxious to make closer contact with the aborigines; it was part of his orders. But the natives were so timid that it took nearly the six weeks of their stay to come to any sort of terms at all. There was plenty of evidence that they were never far away — food left still cooking, footprints in the wet beach below high-water mark, and, very rarely, a sight of the natives. But for a single sailor to approach quite a large group of the natives was hopeless; they were off as quickly as frightened rabbits. Finally Cook decided to treat them like timid, unbroken colts. Get as near as possible without their bolting, then, by taking no notice of them, hope that they would approach the English. The idea worked. Slowly, like scared puppies, they made a snuffling approach, sniffing the air for danger and shouting as if to give themselves courage; then sensing that the proffered hand meant no harm, they came right up. Gifts were showered on them, "which they received without the least sign of satisfaction." If they kept the presents they took no interest in them, sometimes they threw them back, believing it to be a game of catch. But when one of the seamen tossed a fish into their canoe, they "expressed the greatest joy imaginable."

Tupia made great strides towards a more trustful understanding, even persuading the aborigines to lay down their lances, but the extreme apprehensive timidity remained. If any of the English passed between them and their arms they were on their feet in a second. Nothing would persuade them to come more than twenty yards from their canoes, and when an officer approached one of their craft to examine it they could stand it no longer and fled.

Still, it had given the Captain and gentlemen the chance to have a more thorough look at the strange inhabitants of Terra Australis; had given the meticulous Cook the opportunity to note in his journal that they expressed surprise, annoyance, or impatience, he was not sure which, by the words, "Tut-tut, Tut-tut." Whether or not we owe those poetic expressions to the aborigines is of no importance, but the word "tut" has eventually found its immortal niche in the *Oxford Dictionary*. The overwhelming feature of the aborigines was dirt, their bodies and hair were caked with filth — a double annoyance to Cook because he hated filth, and it prevented his arriving at the exact colour of their skin, for they were none too co-operative when he attempted to scrape away a patch of muck from their bodies.

Without exception they were stark naked, frequently painted with broad red and white stripes.

> Their skins were so uniformly covered with dirt, that it was very difficult to ascertain their true colour: we made

> several attempts by wetting our fingers and rubbing it, to remove the incrustations, but with very little effect. With the dirt they appear very nearly as black as a negro, and according to our best discoveries, the skin itself is of the colour of wood soot, or what is commonly called a chocolate colour.

The hair, noted Cook, "is straight, but sometimes it has a slight curl; we saw none that was not matted and filthy." Later the Captain was persuaded to take a second look at their heads and one of the cleaner ones was selected for his inspection. He went over it carefully, finally admitting that the hair was woolly, and though indescribably matted with filth, he was pleased to note, "to our great astonishment, free from lice."

Conversation between British and aborigine was at an absolute premium; they could not understand a single word of each other's language, nor Tupia's. Loud shouting was substituted, though the lack of a common language finally made very little difference, as can be appreciated from this entry in the Captain's journal:

> Their principal ornament is the bone which they thrust through the cartilage that divides the nostrils from each other. What perversion of taste could make them think this a decoration, or what could prompt them, before they had worn it or seen it worn, to suffer the pain and inconvenience that must of necessity attend it, is perhaps beyond the power of human sagacity to determine. As this bone is as thick as a man's finger, and between five and six

> inches long, it reaches quite across the face, and so effectually stops up both the nostrils, that they are forced to keep their mouths wide open for breath, and snuffle so when they attempt to speak, that they are scarcely intelligible even to each other. Our seamen, with some humour, called it their spritsail-yard; and, indeed, it had so ludicrous an appearance, that till we were used to it, we found it difficult to refrain from laughter.

Nose jewels, other members of the crew called them.

It was probably a relief to all that the aborigines refused, or failed to understand an offer to dine on board . . . considering the dirt, smells and snuffles it was brave to issue the invitation. Even the presents they had been given were thrown away. "Mr. Banks found the greater part of the cloth that had been given to them lying in heaps together, probably as useless lumber, not worth carrying away; for they seemed to set very little value upon anything we had except our turtles." And their love for the turtle ended in an ugly incident, finally forcing the British to keep them at a distance, for as they became bolder so they grew into a dangerous nuisance.

One day several of the natives came aboard the ship and seeing some turtles lying on the deck, undoubtedly a great dainty to them, asked for one by signs. Fresh food was the last thing that could be spared, but the refusal of their request put them in a nasty temper. Cook offered them the unpromising alternative of ship's biscuits, which they immediately threw overboard with great disdain — and remarkably sensible of them, too — stamping their feet in transports of resentment and indignation. Then, like wheedling children, they asked everyone in turn for a turtle, but without success; baffled anger quickly followed the wheedling. Rushing across the deck they grasped a couple of turtles, dragging them to the ship's side. With stolid, unhurried strength the seamen quietly replaced the stolen turtles alongside the others. "They would not however relinquish their enterprise, but made several other attempts of the same kind, in all which being equally disappointed, they suddenly leaped into their canoes in a rage and began to paddle towards the shore."

Uncertain of their mood, Cook raced them to the land in his own boat, for he had men working on the beach. As soon as the natives landed they snatched a burning brand from under a pitch kettle, taking the sailors completely by surprise, and running swiftly in a circuit to windward of the English party, set fire to the grass, which was six feet high and as dry as tinder. Within seconds the seamen were surrounded on three sides by a curtain of fire burning with amazing speed and fury; they were in no great danger, for their path to the sea was clear.

Unpredictable as ever, the natives returned in the evening and a kind of truce was negotiated. "As we went along, they told us by signs, that they would not set fire to the grass any more." But two hours later, while squatting on their haunches, apparently quite happy, they suddenly jumped up, dashed for the woods, and started more fires. By the time darkness fell, the hills and country for miles around were blazing violently, "which at night made a most striking and beautiful appearance."

Luckily the blaze had done the English no damage. If the natives had taken it into their heads to start the fires a couple of days earlier, the result would have been a horrible massacre. All their gunpowder was then ashore, a great quantity of valuable stores, instruments, and the sick in tents, who would certainly have been burned to death, so quickly did the fire spread.

> We had no idea of the fury with which grass would burn in this hot climate, nor consequently of the difficulty of extinguishing it; but we determined that if it should ever again be necessary for us to pitch our tents in such a situation, our first measure should be to clear the ground round us.

Naturally, the fishing expedition, the trips inland with Banks, and hunting parties were only interludes to pass away the time till *Endeavour* was repaired and fit for sea. Scanning through Cook's journal for this period, we need not read between the lines to realize that he was a very worried man. He was worried about the state of his ship. He frankly admits that even when they got to sea he was damned if he could make up his mind which way they were going to steer, for from what he had seen of the passage ahead from a hilltop, the navigation looked impossibly dangerous, whatever course he decided on. Lastly, he was apprehensive about the morale of his ship's company if ever they should realize how slim their chances of survival really were. Though he had done all he could to keep them happy, treating everyone, officers and men alike, with a strict impartiality.

> What we caught, as well as the fish, was always equally divided among us by weight, the meanest person on board having the same share as myself; and I think every commander in such a voyage as this, will find it to his interest to follow the same rule.

Had Captain Bligh, an officer who in later years served under Cook, followed that sound advice, the mutiny in his ship might well have been avoided.

Endeavour's bows were now patched up, but already three unsuccessful attempts had been made to refloat her, each one a manoeuvre taking days of preparation. With the fourth try they were successful but she had been floating only a few minutes before it was obvious that the awkward position in which she had lain — bows ashore, stern floating — had strained her badly amidships, causing another serious leak and leaving the Captain no option but to go through the tedious operation of laying his ship back on shore. He was still not certain of the condition of *Endeavour's* stern, and this brief sentence shows how careful he had to be with the morale of his men. "I got one of the carpenter's crew, a man in whom I could confide, to go down again to the ship's bottom, and examine the place." Fortunately her stern was in fairly good condition, but it is obvious that the seaman selected for the survey had to be a man who could hold his tongue; wild rumours would spread through the ship's company with the speed of a bush fire.

All these were no more than trivial, irritating difficulties compared to the main problem. What was going to happen once, and if, they got to sea? Cook knew their only chance lay in threading a way north through the tangled coral reefs, for the wind blew constantly from the south, and a return home by the route they had come, beating back into the wind, frequently blowing at gale force, for 2000 miles amid the hazards of reef and shoal, was completely, hopelessly impossible. It was north or nothing. But what a terrifying prospect loomed ahead.

> I went myself upon a hill, which lies over the south point, to take a view of the sea. At this time it was low water, and I saw, with great concern, innumerable sandbanks and shoals lying all along the coast in every direction. The innermost lay about three or four miles from the shore, the outermost extended as far as I could see with my glass, and many of them did not but just rise above the water. There was some appearance of a passage to the northward, and I had no hope of getting clear but in that direction.

Consequently, the Master was sent out day after day in a boat to take soundings and see if he could discover the start of a passage to the northward, getting as far as twenty to twenty-five miles from the ship. On occasions his reports were hopeful, sometimes not, but finally, "the Master returned with the discouraging account that there was no passage for the ship to northward." Cook shrugged his shoulders; it made no difference, that was their only escape route. It would have been just the same to tell a man in a burning room with the door blocked that he must not jump out of the window.

Under the pretense of going for a stroll along the beach, Cook and Banks went ashore,

> but chiefly to indulge an anxious curiosity by looking round us upon the sea, of which our wishes almost persuaded us, we had formed an idea more disadvantageous than the truth. After having walked about seven miles along the shore to the northward, we ascended a very high hill, and were soon convinced that the danger of our situation was at least equal to our apprehension; for in whatever direction we turned our eyes, we saw rocks and shoals without number, and no passage out to sea but through the winding channels between them, which could not be navigated without the last degree of difficulty and danger. We returned therefore to the ship, not in better spirits than when we left it.

It might have been more appropriate if the Captain had taken his Master or the First Lieutenant with him and confided in them, men with years of seafaring experience, instead of young Joseph Banks. But between those two — Cook, the seasoned mariner, Captain of *Endeavour* solely through his own self-taught efforts, and Banks, passenger aboard the ship because of his wealth, gentle birth, and influential connections (it was only incidental that he was, too, a brilliant botanist) — there had grown up the respect of two men who recognized in the other a brave, staunch friend. They both could look dispassionately at the almost insurmountable dangers ahead, look each other in the eye and admit their chances of survival were as delicate as a spider's web. Basically they were the same, and beside that, the wide difference of birth and upbringing meant nothing at all.

By the beginning of August they were ready for sea, waiting for the weather to moderate and the water across the bar of the harbour to deepen sufficiently to let them out; but they never seemed to come right at the same time, either there was a sufficient depth of water and a howling gale stopped them, or it was the other way round. At last, at five o'clock in the morning of the 4th of August, they passed over the bar and got under sail.

Overhead it was grey and hazy, and a steady monotonous rain fell. The day before the carpenter had examined the pumps and "to our great mortification found them all in a state of decay." No pumps, no protective sheathing, false keel gone, food stocks perilously low, and before them the dreaded teeth of the Great Barrier Reef, a vicious enemy that had already tasted their blood.

> A little before noon we anchored in fifteen fathoms of water, with a sandy bottom; for I did not think it safe to run in amongst the shoals till I had well viewed them at low water from the mast-head, which might determine me which way to steer; for, as yet, I was in doubt whether I should beat back to the southward, round all the shoals, or seek a passage to the eastward or to the northward, all which at present appeared to be equally difficult and dangerous.
>
> To the harbour which we had now left, I gave the name of Endeavour River.

XIII

BACK ON THE MAP

August–September, 1770

AT LOW-WATER I went to the mast-head and took a view of the shoals which made a very threatening appearance." Indeed, as far as the eye could see, the ocean was studded with hundreds of islands. On his west side the mainland of Australia; north and south, innumerable reefs; and to the east, the outside edge of the Great Barrier Reef, on which the might of the Pacific hurled itself with a thunderous, exploding surf, bursting skywards in a glittering fan of silver spray.

The problem was resolving itself for Cook into two constructive alternatives and one final expedient. First, to try to force a way through to the north inside the reef. Second, if this proved impossible, to get right outside the reef; and if both these failed, to turn about and thread a tortuous course home the way they had come. But it is easy to detect a strong feeling among the officers that they would prefer the third experiment, namely, to turn round and go home the way they had come, without attempting the first two alternatives. The Master had already expressed the opinion that there was no way through to the north. Here it is well to remember that it was the officers who had urged Cook to return home via the coast of New Holland

and Batavia, believing the general condition of the ship unlikely to stand up to the strains of a return home round South America. This reversal of their former ideas, this wish to turn back, allows us to look northward through the very eyes of those men, for the navigational horrors they could see ahead now convinced them that their only, extremely slender, hope of survival lay in returning home by their outward route. Let us remember, too, that the Captain could see the terrible dangers ahead if they persisted in their present course — could see them just as plainly as his men.

Whenever there was a doubt about their future policy Cook generally called a conference of his officers, to see if he could detect a feeling of uncertainty among them as to the rightness of his intended action. He had allowed himself to be swayed by them when they left New Zealand, for his inclinations had been to return home by South America. There was nothing weak in this attitude, it was the action of a man with an open, clear mind. If he thought the alternatives of his officers reasonable, in fact likely to be of more service to the Royal Navy and his country, he adopted them. "These anxious deliberations engaged us till eleven o'clock at night." But this time the Captain decided his own policy was correct: they would go north.

Their progress was painfully slow, Cook giving his steering direction from the masthead, always with a boat ahead to give forewarning of danger. It was only safe to venture forward when the tide was practically out, exposing the reefs, and frequently, when the tide was right, the wind blew at gale force, making movement impossible; or again, tide and wind were right but visibility too hazy to allow progress. At such times Cook would call from the masthead for some of the officers to come aloft. There they would sit among the mist-drenched sails and sheet vainly straining their eyes for sight of a way out.

> Myself, with several of the officers, kept a look-out at the mast-head to see if any passage could be discovered between the shoals, but nothing was in view except the breakers . . . through the labyrinth formed by these shoals, I was altogether at a loss which way to steer.

After a time they thought they could detect a clear opening before them and hoped they were once more out of danger; "in this hope, however, we soon found ourselves disappointed, and for that reason I called the headland Cape Flattery." They steered along the shore until one o'clock for what they thought was an open channel, when the petty officer at the masthead cried out that he could see land stretching menacingly right across their path, and between the ship and the mainland, another reef.

> Upon this I ran to the mast-head myself, from whence I very plainly saw the reef, which was now so far to windward, that we could not weather it, but the land ahead which he had supposed to be the main, appeared to me to be only a cluster of islands. As soon as I got down from the mast-head, the master and some others went up (only too willing to put the worst construction on the danger and turn back) who all insisted that the land ahead was

not islands, but the main, and to make their report still more alarming, they said that they saw breakers all round us.

Whether the obstacle ahead was mainland or islands, Cook was not prepared to turn back without investigating what lay beyond. He anchored for the night and went forward the next day, "in the pinnace, accompanied by Mr. Banks, whose fortitude and curiosity made him a party in every expedition." The Captain did not want the pessimistic chatter of his officers; Joseph Banks was the ideal companion, the sort of sympathetic friend to whom Cook could think aloud and express his doubts, knowing that Banks was not waiting to fan the slightest smoulder of indecision, and urge him to turn back, as his officers would. About one o'clock they reached the loftiest of the islands "and immediately ascended the highest hill, with a mixture of hope and fear, proportioned to the importance of our business, and the uncertainty of the event." When they looked round they could see reefs and islands stretching out of sight with the ocean swell breaking in a dreadful surf, "and I conceived hopes of getting without these, as I perceived several breaks or openings in the reef and deep water between." A hazy blanket of mist hung over everything, and though they remained on the island all day the weather never really cleared. Cook decided to stop for the night and hope for a brighter day on the morrow, and finding a bush on the beach that afforded some shelter, he and Banks lay down to sleep. At three in the morning Cook sent off a mate in the pinnace to investigate a gap in the reef, but he returned full of pessimism, shouting wolf before he was bitten. It was too narrow, the wind blew too hard, the tide raced too fast; "this however did not discourage me, for I judged from his description of the place he had been at that he had seen it to disadvantage."

The Captain returned on board determined to get outside rather than "run the risk of being locked in by the great reef," and to keep pressing northwards in the hopes that a few days' sailing might see the end of the reef and a speedier passage to the East Indies, "as we now had but little more than three months provision on board at short allowance."

The next morning Cook placed his ship abreast a gap in the reef while the Master went ahead to make a final check. Through this opening the tide rushed with a smooth, oily speed, narrowing to the characteristic V-shape of fast-flowing water. Either side of this "eye in the needle" rose the sharp teeth of coral. Cook was taking a calculated risk; when the moment came to shoot the gap he would have no control over his ship. He waited quietly, received the Master's "go-ahead" signal, and aimed the bows of *Endeavour* for the middle of the gap. The tide gripped her and she shot through like a cork in a millrace . . . into deep, bottomless water, cradled on a huge swell rolling in from the southeast.

> Our change of circumstance was now visible on every countenance, for it was most sensibly felt in every breast: we had been little less than three months entangled amongst the shoals and rocks, that every moment threatened us with destruction; frequently passing our night at anchor within hearing of the surge that broke over them: sometimes driving towards them even while our anchors were out, and knowing that if by any accident, to

which an almost continual tempest exposed us, they should not hold, we must in a few minutes inevitably perish. But now, after sailing no less than one thousand and eighty miles, without once having a man out of the chains heaving the lead, even for a minute, which perhaps never happened to any other vessel, (for most of that time too, one and sometimes three boats constantly ahead sounding) we found ourselves in an open sea, with deep water; and enjoyed a flow of spirits, which was equally owing to our late danger and our present security.

That night Cook stood well out to sea but the next morning came back towards the coast, "in order to get within sight of land, that I might be sure not to overshoot the passage; if passage there was, between this land and New Guinea" (the elusive Torres Strait).

Now they found themselves in worse danger than when they were inside the reef, for the moment the wind dropped and the tide started to flow towards the land, they were carried inexorably towards the reef.

> About four o'clock in the morning we plainly heard the roaring of the surf and at break of day saw it foaming to a vast height, at not more than a mile's distance. Our distress now returned upon us with double force; the waves which rolled in upon the reef, carried us towards it very fast; we could reach no ground with an anchor and had not a breath of wind for the sails."

All three boats were out ahead desperately trying to pull

Endeavour away from the danger, but losing ground rapidly, and at six o'clock that evening they were only a "hundred yards from the rocks upon which the same billow which washed the side of the ship, broke to a tremendous height the very next time it rose; so that between us and destruction there was only a dreary valley, no wider than the base of one wave."

This time it seemed their luck was at an end, there was no escape. But a gentle breeze sprang up, "so light that at any other time we should not have observed it," and gave the men pulling in the boats just that tiny bit of help which enabled them to get clear.

A mile ahead they could see a narrow opening in the reef and all their hopes were centred on getting back inside, but the breeze that had helped them temporarily for ten miles, dropped, and they were rushed back towards the rocks. Again, when they were no more than a stone's throw from destruction, a scarcely perceptible breeze sprang up, and by its help they got *Endeavour* opposite the gap, just as the tide turned. Instead of being swept through, she was hustled two miles out to sea on the current. It gave them a temporary break, a chance to regain their breath, but only until the tide turned. Then they were sucked back towards the rocks; this time a little farther north, but again opposite a gap in the coral. "We struggled hard with the flood, sometimes gaining a little and sometimes losing, but every man still did his duty."

Then carried irresistibly on the powerful current, which but for the opening in the rocks would have smashed them to matchwood on the coral, they were swept back inside the reef with "amazing rapidity, by a torrent that kept us from driving against either side of the channel."

> And now, such is the vicissitude of life, we thought ourselves happy in having regained a situation which, but two days before, it was the utmost object of our hope to quit. Rocks and shoals are always dangerous to the mariner, even where their situation has been ascertained; they are more dangerous in seas which have never before been navigated, and in this part of the globe they are more dangerous than in any other: for here there are reefs and coral rocks, rising like a wall almost perpendicular out of the unfathomable deep . . . and here the enormous waves of the vast Southern Ocean meeting with so abrupt a resistance, break with inconceivable violence.

Once again within the comparative safety of the reef, Cook dropped the anchor, and looking towards the gap in the coral through which his ship had been sucked with such force and speed, he wondered at their good fortune in being afloat at all. "Providential Channel" he named it.

He was now certain their only course was northwards, inside the reef, for during their brief spell outside another unpleasant fact had been forced on him: "we could not safely put the same confidence in our vessel as before she had struck: for the blows she had received had so widened her leaks, that she admitted no less than nine inches of water an hour." This, without pumps, and "the danger of navigating in unknown parts of the ocean was now greatly increased by our having a crazy ship." Their survival lay in moving forward with even more caution than before. Two boats were kept constantly sounding ahead, examining every foot of the way, and if the minutest doubt arose, the ship was anchored, however long it might take to find the next stretch of clear water; and though they were surrounded by danger, a new confidence was felt aboard. "We were now encompassed on every side: but having lately been exposed to much greater danger, and rocks and shoals being grown familiar, we looked at them comparatively with little concern."

For nearly three weeks *Endeavour* moved steadily forward, but as the end of her appalling ordeal approached, she did not burst suddenly into the freedom of the Indian Ocean. The coast started to trend westward, the soundings became more regular, until, passing between two points, "we could see no land, so that we conceived hopes of having at last, found a passage into the Indian Sea." Cook landed on one of the numerous islands and, climbing to the highest point, knew that Torres Strait was no myth,

> which gave me great satisfaction, not only because the dangers and fatigues of the voyage were drawing to an end, but because it would no longer be in doubt whether Australia and New Guinea were two separate islands.
>
> As I was now about to quit the eastern coast of New Holland, which I had coasted from latitude thirty eight degrees to this place, and which I am confident no European had ever seen before, I once more hoisted the English colours, and though I had already taken possession of several particular parts, now took possession of

the whole eastern coast, from latitude thirty eight degrees to this place, latitude ten and a half South, in the right of his Majesty King George the third, by the name of New South Wales, with all the bays, harbours, rivers and islands situated upon it: we then fired three volleys of small arms, which were answered by the same number from the ship. Having performed this ceremony upon the island, we named it Possession Island.

Cook now had time to sum up in his usual modest and generous way his impressions of Australia. He praised Green's work wholeheartedly: "it would be injurious to Mr. Green, not to take this opportunity of attesting that he was indefatigable both in making observations and calculating upon them. . . . " Quite fifty per cent of the work was Cook's. He was grateful, too, for the way Green had found time to instruct his petty officers in the art of navigation and crisply notes in his journal that it would be a great benefit to the Navy if "observing and calculating were considered necessary qualifications for every sea officer."

Though Cook had only travelled up the eastern coast — nevertheless, a distance amounting to nearly 2000 miles in a straight line — he was sure Australia was "of a larger extent than any other country in the known world, . . . and that its square surface must be much more than equal to all Europe." Then he makes an uncannily accurate remark, "but there is great reason to believe that this immense tract is either wholly desolate, or at least still more thinly inhabited than the parts we visited," basing that assumption on a clear, undeniable fact, so obvious that ninety-nine out of a hundred would overlook it. If there were people living inland then they could not "subsist without cultivations: it is extremely improbable that the inhabitants of the coast should be totally ignorant of the arts of cultivation which were practiced inland; and it is equally improbable that if they knew such arts, there should be no traces of them among them."

Very simple, but true.

Of the aborigines he noted that they neither traded nor were they thieves, facts which he did not believe greatly to their credit, for they had not the wit or imagination to do either. They lived in huts inferior to a bird's nest and far from adequate: "they were just high enough for a man to sit upright in, but not large enough for him to extend himself in his whole length in any direction." A most extraordinary shelter to build and, unfortunately, there seems to be no record as to whether they lay with their feet warm inside and their heads exposed, or vice versa. "The only tools we saw among them are an adze wretchedly made of stone." In conclusion Cook wrote, "I have faithfully related facts, the reader must judge for himself."

At last, after a year and a week, *Endeavour* was back on the map. She had made a great sweeping arc into the unknown, uncharted ocean of the South Pacific, the last four months of which had strained the nerves, minds, and bodies of them all beyond the prudent limit of human endurance. But now, released from the horrors of the Great Barrier Reef, they felt free as birds. They could cram on all canvas and sail along the western shore of New Guinea in long, unhindered tacks, making for Batavia. It was essential to reach a harbour with dockyard facilities as soon as possible: the ship was in a leaky condition and stores were very low.

Cook landed once on the coast of New Guinea, hoping to obtain fresh fruit, but he and his party were dangerously opposed by the natives, who used a curious weapon: "the foremost threw something out of his hand, which flew on one side of him, and burnt exactly like gunpowder but made no report."

Fruit there was in plenty, but it was not in Cook's nature to start a fight in which the natives were bound to fare worst, "for two or three hundred green coconuts, which would at most have procured us a mere transient gratification." He retreated to the safety of his boat, satisfying himself with a close study of the inhabitants from the safety of the pinnace, "though we looked at the fruit very wistfully." The natives marched along the shore, shouting their defiance,

> and letting off their fires by four or five at a time. What these fires were, or for what purpose intended, we could not imagine: those who discharged them had in their hands a short piece of stick, possibly a hollow cane, which they swung sideways from them, and we immediately saw fire and smoke, exactly resembling those of a musket, and of no longer duration. This wonderful phenomenon was observed from the ship, and the deception was so great, that the people on board thought they had firearms.

These firearms do not appear to have been noticed by any other navigator and were probably blowpipes, used by the Papuans, the inhabitants of that part of New Guinea. This serves to show how amazing stories were brought back by sailors returning home from foreign parts, the sailors quite genuinely believing in what they imagined they had seen. Inaccuracy hurt James Cook; yet even he thought the natives were armed with some sort of firearm. It is easy to see how a seaman with a slightly vivid imagination could create and believe in mermaids, giants, and the huge goblins supposed to exist in the South Seas. A dim light, an extra tot or two of rum, an indistinct shadow seen on the beach, a description passing from mouth to mouth and getting a little more distorted each time, and we have the legendary "frightful Colossus" of South America.

Soon after returning to the ship the boat was hoisted in and they made sail to the westward, determined to press on for Batavia as fast as possible, "to the great satisfaction of a very considerable majority of the ship's company." The men were restless, anxious to be on their way, homesick. Banks noted they "were pretty far gone with a longing for home which the physicians have gone so far as to esteem a disease under the name of nostalgia." But not so the officers, whom Cook rebuked sternly. "I am sorry to say that I was strongly urged by some of the officers to send a party of men ashore to cut down the coconut trees for the sake of the fruit. To this I peremptorily refused, as equally unjust and cruel."

This appears to be making an undue fuss over a few coconuts, but the reasons were sincere and of a practical necessity. Obviously, if the Papuans had resisted their landing when they had not attempted to take anything, they would resist a foraging raid much more strongly, "in which case many of them must have fallen a sacrifice to our attempt, and perhaps also some of our own people . . . it would have been highly criminal."

In addition, Cook suspected they were in the terrain of the Dutch East India Company and he did not want a diplomatic upset with a nation he hoped soon to ask for essential repairs to his ship, to get them home. It is only necessary to think back to *Endeavour's* prolonged and unpleasant stay at Rio de Janeiro on the way out, to see how touchy the outposts of European colonies could be if they had reason to think their diplomatic rights and charters were being interfered with. Nor was it necessary for these colonists to have a genuine reason. It was the shining fat pieces of gold that could be slipped discreetly into the administrator's pocket which really made them jealous of their power. *Endeavour* was back on the map and Cook was not going to forget it.

For nearly a fortnight he sailed west along the coast, hindered by strong contrary currents to the southward, slowing down progress to as little as ten and even six miles in a day's sailing. Then, on the 17th of September, "being clear of all islands which are laid down in the maps we had on board," an island suddenly popped up on the horizon to the southwest, where it had no business to be. "At first I thought we had made a new discovery"; but it was no more than a very typical piece of earlier chart work from the good old days when explorers collected little pieces of land and scattered them about their charts with an abandon usually associated with the pepperpot: "none of the islands that we have seen in these seas are placed within a reasonable distance of their true situation."

Cook steered directly for the island and by ten o'clock was close enough in to see houses, coconut trees,

> and to our very agreeable surprise, numerous flocks of sheep; this was a temptation not to be resisted by people in our situation, especially as many of us were in a bad state of health, and many still repining at my not having touched at Timor: it was therefore soon decided to attempt a commerce with the people who appeared to be so well able to supply our many necessities, and remove at once the sickness and discontent that had got footing amongst us.

This showed an almost unprecedented amount of thought for his men, for quite a few captains would ignore even physical sickness until it was absolutely forced on them, and by that time the only effective action they could take was to stitch the corpse in canvas and commit it to the sea with the minimum of ceremony. For a captain to worry himself about symptoms of discontent in his ship's company, or even to go so far as to admit they had minds with which to be discontented, was something new. Cook's thought for the health and happiness of his men was revolutionary and, consequently, he had difficulty in convincing his officers of the importance of tying up health — mental and physical — with the efficiency of the ship.

On his second voyage, when he commanded two ships, he in the *Resolution* and Captain Furneaux in the *Adventure,* he was not able to convince even his second-in-command of the success of his own antiscorbutic methods and the importance of insisting that the crew use them.

I sent on board the *Adventure* to inquire into the state of her crew, having heard that they were sickly, and this I now found was but too true; her cook was dead and about twenty of her best men were down in the scurvy and flux. At this time, we had only three men on the sick list [though Cook had been at sea nearly two months longer than Furneaux] and only one of them attacked with the scurvy. To introduce any new article of food among seamen, let it be ever so much for their good, requires both the example and authority of a commander; without both of which it will be dropped before the people are sensible of the benefit resulting from it: were it necessary I could name fifty instances in support of this remark. I appointed one of my seamen to be cook for the *Adventure* and wrote to Captain Furneaux, desiring him to make use of every method to stop the spreading of the disease amongst his people.

If Cook could not trust an officer directly under his command to carry out simple instructions for the physical health of the crew, it is certain that such old-fashioned things as homesickness and Banks's modern "nostalgia" took up no part of the average captain's time in those rough, tough days. But of course, Cook was years ahead of his contemporaries.

However, to return to the tempting contemplation of the sheep ashore — already roasted realities to the salt-sickened palates of the men — the pinnace was lowered and Lieutenant

Gore headed the party ashore in search of fresh provisions. Unable to make anything of the native chatter, he returned to the ship. The Captain sent him in a second time accompanied by Solander, while *Endeavour,* not finding an anchorage, stood on and off from the coast, viewing with amazement two horsemen on the hills, dressed in European clothes. Soon they received a signal from Gore informing them there was safe anchorage in the next bay and they made towards it. Just as the boat's crew were shoving off from the beach, "the horsemen in European dress came up, but Lieutenant Gore, not having his commission about him, thought it best to decline a conference." This illustrates again how extremely careful they had to be not to arouse suspicion. At the root of their necessary caution was the absence of any form of communication with a higher authority for instruction, should some tricky diplomatic problem arise, for it would take months, even years, to get a reply back.

That evening they anchored in a small bay opposite a large native town, and ashore the Dutch colours could be seen. The next morning Gore was sent ashore to get in touch with some responsible person and obtain stores. He was escorted into the town by a motley guard of natives armed with muskets so rusted up that the triggers could not be pulled. He was introduced to the Rajah of the island and a representative of the Dutch East India Company, a half-caste with the impressive name of Johan Christopher Lange. It was explained that nothing could be sold until permission was obtained from a gentleman who lived a little way inland, but that in the meantime Mr. Lange and the Rajah would like to dine aboard. "Mr. Gore intimated that he was ready to attend them." Again, this caution: "they desired that two of our people might be left ashore as hostages: and in this also they were indulged."

At two o'clock they all sat down to a dinner of roast mutton, an extravagance they would not have dreamed of had it not been for the sight of the sheep ashore, and after Cook had convinced the Rajah that he thought it a privilege to have him at his table; for "he seemed to hesitate, and at last, with some confusion, said he did not imagine that we, who were white men, would suffer him, who was of a different colour, to sit down in our company," an idea implanted in his head by the half-caste Lange, who turned out to be a detestable creature. During the meal the Rajah said how much he would like to own an English sheep and Cook gave him the only one left aboard. Encouraged, he asked for an English dog. "Mr. Banks politely gave up his greyhound. Mr. Lange then intimated that a spying glass would be acceptable, and one was immediately put into his hands." In return, they promised the Captain that on the morrow he might purchase as much livestock as he wished; "this put us all in high spirits, and the liquor circulated rather faster than either the Indian or the Saxon could bear; they intimated their desire to go away before they were quite drunk."

Early next morning Cook landed to buy his livestock, but one excuse followed another, and by the middle of the afternoon not even a chicken had been offered for sale. Hot, annoyed at the waste of time, hungry,

> and very unwilling to return on board and eat salt provisions, where so many delicacies surrounded us ashore,

we petitioned his majesty for permission to purchase a small hog and some rice, and to employ his subjects to dress them. He answered very graciously, that if we could eat victuals dressed by his subjects, which he could scarcely suppose, he would do himself the honour of entertaining us. We expressed our gratitude and immediately sent on board for some liquor. About five o'clock, dinner was ready; it was served in six-and-thirty dishes, or rather baskets, containing alternately rice and pork; and three earthenware bowls, filled with the liquor in which the pork had been boiled: these were ranged upon the floor, and mats laid round them for us to sit upon. We were then conducted by turns to a hole in the floor, near which stood a man with water in a vessel, made of the leaves of the fan palm, who assisted us in washing our hands. When this was done, we placed ourselves round the victuals, and waited for the king. As he did not come, we inquired for him, and were told that the custom of the country did not permit the person who gave the entertainment to sit down with his guests; but that, if we suspected the victuals to be poisoned, he would come down and taste it. We immediately declared that we had no such suspicion, and desired that none of the rituals of hospitality might be violated on our account. The prime minister and Mr. Lange were of our party and we made a most luxurious meal: we thought the pork and rice excellent, and the broth not to be despised; but the spoons, which were made of leaves, were so small, that few of us had patience to use them. After dinner, our wine passed briskly about, and we again inquired for our royal host, thinking that though the custom of his country would not allow him to eat with us, he might at least share in the jollity of our bottle; but he again excused himself, saying that the master of a feast should never be drunk, which there was no certain way to avoid but by not tasting the liquor. As wine generally warms and opens the heart, we took an opportunity, when we thought its influence began to be felt, to revive the subject of the buffaloes and sheep, of which we had not in all this time heard a syllable, though they were to have been brought down early in the morning.

But though Mr. Lange had drunk his share of the wine, he was not too far gone to invent another string of excuses, coupled with a great many trivial conditions of sale, which Cook believed were only included so that the English were almost certain to break some of them and give Lange the chance to fine them for disregarding the conditions of sale. However, an assurance was given that the next day they would be able to buy as much livestock as they wanted. But Cook was angry, very angry; in his eyes a heinous crime had been committed. A market pact had been broken. To Cook, brought up in the traditions of a market town, where the shake of a hand was an unbreakable bond, the action of Mr. Lange, who considered himself a European was unforgivable. "We all returned on board very much dissatisfied with the issue of our negotiations."

The next morning they were on the beach. No Lange, no cattle, no sheep, just a half-caste Portuguese claiming to be Lange's assistant, a great many discontented natives, most anxious to sell their livestock, a fuming, furious Captain, and the ancient native prime minister who had dined with them the night before. To add to the Captain's wrath: "I saw, to my great astonishment, Dr. Solander, quite unmoved, coming from the town, followed by above a hundred men, some armed with muskets and some with lances."

It was too much. Cook decided to have no further dealings with Lange, and approached the old prime minister.

> I took him by the hand, and presented him with an old broad sword. This instantly turned the scales in our favour; he received the sword with a transport of joy, and flourishing it over the busy Portuguese, who crouched like a fox to a lion, he made him and the officer who commanded the party, sit down upon the ground behind him.

Trade then proceeded briskly, fairly, and entirely to the Captain's satisfaction:

> . . . we might have bought as much as would have freighted our ship. The refreshment which we procured here consisted of wine, buffaloes, six sheep, three hogs, thirty dozen fowls, a few limes and some coco-nuts; many dozen of eggs, half of which, however, proved to be rotten, a little garlic, and several hundred gallons of palm-syrup.

The latter commodity caused Cook some unnecessary worry. "We were at first afraid that the syrup, of which some of our people ate very great quantities, would have brought on the fluxes, but its aperient qualities were so slight, that what effect it produced was rather salutary than hurtful."

Ironically, one of Cook's first remarks on sighting the island of Savu, and seeing horsemen apparently dressed as Europeans, had been: "by this we knew that the place had been settled by Europeans and that the many disagreeable circumstances which always attend the first establishment of commerce with savages, would be avoided."

Two years among savages must have dimmed his memory, so to Mr. Lange must go the credit of bringing the Captain back to the realities of civilized commerce. Cook needed only three words to describe the representative of the Dutch East India Company — "crafty and iniquitous."

To Cook, the native population had one bad and one good point. They possessed a pernicious habit of chewing a mixture of tobacco, lime, betel nuts, and areca from a very young age, "so that their mouths are disgustful in the highest degree both to the smell and the sight; the tobacco taints their breath and the betel and lime make the teeth not only as black as charcoal, but as rotten too."

But with his fanatical worship of cleanliness, he had to call on the goddess of sewers to do justice to their sanitary arrangements.

> In one instance, their delicacy and cleanliness are very remarkable. Many of us were ashore here three successive days, from a very early hour in the morning till it was dark, yet we never saw the least trace of an offering to Cloacina, nor could we so much as guess where they were made. In a country so populous this is very difficult to be accounted for; and perhaps there is no other country in the world where the secret is so effectually kept.

XIV

FAREWELL TO THE SOUTH SEAS

September, 1770 – June, 1771

BATAVIA: the heart of the Dutch East India trading company, the city of disease and death, and *Endeavour's* first real contact with the known world after two and a half years in the unknown.

A few days before their expected time of arrival, Cook called his ship's company together to impress on them the absolute secrecy of their voyage and to take into his possession the journals and diaries of the officers, petty officers, and seamen, "at least all I could find." That night, as a sultry tropical thunder rolled over the ocean, they saw by the vivid flashes of lightning land, bearing to the east. Below decks, poor Tupia, the gentle, cultured Tahitan, tossed feverishly in his hammock, a very sick man.

Hindered by contrary currents and light winds they moved slowly towards the harbour. Ahead lay two Dutch ships, positive links with Europe. "I sent Mr. Hicks on board one of them to enquire news of our country, from which we had been absent so long. From them we heard with great pleasure, that the *Swallow* had been at Batavia about two years before." This was Captain Carteret's gallant little ship, presumed lost. She had sailed with Wallis on the expedition immediately preceding Cook's and had not reached England when *Endeavour* sailed. Bougainville, too, in the *Boudeause,* had touched at Batavia a few months later. In London, they were told, the mob had rioted with cries of "Down with King George! King Wilkes for ever." And from the American colonies came the alarming news of near open rebellion to the old country; they were refusing to pay their taxes.

Soon the forms and formalities of a busy port started, and the inevitable questions were asked, for after the two years' hammering *Endeavour* had taken, with only the crudest of repairs possible, she looked like a tired old prizefighter, bruised and battered. Mr. Hicks was asked to write in a book the name of the ship and where she had come from. Very deliberately he wrote, "from Europe." The Dutch officer raised his eyebrows, glanced quizzically round the deck, "but said he was satisfied with anything we thought fit to write, it being intended merely for the information of those who should enquire after us from motives of friendship."

This was followed by a form containing nine questions, "very ill expressed," says Cook, and so they were. The last is typical of them: "If any other news worth of attention, at the place from whence the ship lastly departed, or during the voyage is happened." Of these questions Cook answered two: the nation to which the ship belonged and where she was going.

Batavia had a bad reputation for its unhealthy climate and the boarding officer with his party seemed a strong confirmation:

they were as pale as spectres, a sad presage of our suffer-

> ing in so unhealthy a country; but our people, who except Tupia, were all rosy and plump, seemed to think themselves so seasoned by various climates that nothing could hurt them.

Through the day the men sweated under the leaden sky of a tropical wet season, a sticky, damp, clammy heat. As dusk began to fall thunder rolled somberly over the country, broken by flashes of lightning. Cook, anticipating the harm such storms could do to his riggings, made lightning conductors of chain running down from the mastheads to the sea. One night, about nine o'clock, a tempest broke over them with incredible violence, the skies seemed to split with the fury of the storm, the rain lashed down in torrents and wicked tongues of forked lightning snaked down with an

> explosion that shook us like an earthquake, the chain at the same time appearing like a line of fire: a sentinel was in the action of charging his piece, and the shock forced the musket out of his hand and broke the rammer rod.

Barely forty feet from them, the masts of a Dutch East Indiaman were struck and split, shivered to pieces. "In all probability we should have shared the same fate as the Dutchman had it not been for the electrical chains. This incident alone is sufficient to recommend these chains to all ships whatever." It was in fact more than half a century later that the Navy accepted Cook's recommendation.

Cook's main reason for calling at Batavia was to get his ship into dry dock, knowing that without extensive repairs, she would never get them home. With this in view he called on the Governor-General, was courteously received, and after a few slight delays *Endeavour* was laid ashore. When the full extent of the damage was revealed they stood aghast, appalled, incredulous that she had got them so far. Great chunks of her bottom had been torn off, everywhere the worm had made disastrous inroads, and in places the planks were

> so worn, that they were not an eighth-part of an inch thick, and here the worms had made their way quite into the timbers; yet in this condition she had sailed many hundreds of miles, where navigation is as dangerous as in any part of the world: how much misery did we escape by being ignorant that so considerable a part of the bottom of the vessel was thinner than the sole of a shoe, and that every life on board depended on so slight and fragile a barrier between us and the unfathomable ocean.

In the meantime, Cook took advantage of the sailing of a Dutch ship to Europe to forward to Mr. Stephenson, the Secretary to the Admiralty, a copy of his journal and such charts as were ready. He accompanied them with a letter, so typically modest, so full of praise for the scientific staff, officers, and men that without knowing of the terrific voyage he had accomplished, one would think he was describing a trip round the harbour.

> I have with undisguised truth and without gloss inserted the whole transactions of the voyage, and have made such remarks and given such descriptions of things

as I thought was necessary in the best manner I was capable of. Although the discoveries made in this voyage are not great, I flatter myself they are such as may merit the attention of their Lordships. Although I have failed in discovering the so much talked of southern continent, which perhaps [does] not exist, and which I myself have much at heart, yet I am confident that no part of the failure of such discovery can be laid to my charge; had we been so fortunate not to have run ashore, much more would have been done in the latter part of the voyage than what was; but as it is, I presume this voyage will be found as complete as any before made to the South Seas on the same account.

In justice to the officers and the whole crew, I must say they have gone through the fatigues and dangers of the whole voyage, with that cheerfulness and alertness that will always do honour to the British seamen, and I have the satisfaction to say that I have not lost one man from sickness during the whole voyage.

But almost within hours of writing those words, "I have not lost one man from sickness," Cook watched with a great bitterness and sorrow his men, his splendid ship's company, succumbing to the dreadful climate of Batavia. "By this time, having been here only nine days, we began to feel the fatal effects of the climate and situation." Against malaria and dysentery the Captain was helpless; he had none of the modern weapons to fight the diseases. He had fought the dreaded scurvy; his vigilance among the perils of unknown seas had saved their lives many times over, but now he was opposed by an enemy beyond his power and knowledge. His men sickened and died. But from Cook's description of Batavia, with its filth, malaria, mosquito-ridden canals, its slaves, the fatalistic attitude to death of the inhabitants, and the terrible climate that drove men mad to run amok in the street, it is not surprising that *Endeavour's* crew, who had survived two years in unexplored oceans, succumbed to two months of this cesspit of the East.

The wet season was just setting in and gnats and mosquitos "swarmed from every plash of water like bees from a hive." From the filthy ditches innumerable frogs croaked a warning of the next sloshing downpour of rain with a noise "ten times louder than any frog in Europe . . . an incessant noise that was almost intolerable." There were few streets without a canal running through them,

> or rather stagnating in them, which in the dry season exhaled a suffocating stench. In the wet season the inconvenience is equal, for then these reservoirs of corrupted water overflow their banks in the lower part of the town, especially in the neighbourhood of the hotels, and fill the lower stories of the houses, where they leave behind them an inconceivable quantity of slime and filth: yet these canals are sometimes cleaned; but the cleaning of them is so managed as to become as great a nuisance as the foulness of the water: for the black mud that is taken from the bottom is suffered to lie upon the banks, that is, in the middle of the street, till it has acquired a sufficient degree of hardness to be loaded in a boat and carried away. As this mud consists chiefly of human ordure, which

> is regularly thrown into the canal every morning, there not being a necessary-house in the whole town, it poisons the air while it is drying to a considerable extent. Even the running streams become nuisances in their turn, by the nastiness or negligence of the people: for every now and then a dead hog, or a dead horse, is stranded upon the shallow place, and it being the business of no particular person to remove the nuisance, it is negligently left to time and accident. While we were here, a dead buffalo lay upon the shoal of a river that ran through one of the principal streets, above a week, and at last was carried away by a flood.

A man-made paradise for mosquitoes, a perfect breeding ground; no wonder Cook says,

> . . . in this country delay is death. In less than a week we were sensible of the unhealthiness of the climate: and in less than a month half the ship's company were unable to do their duty. We were told that of a hundred soldiers who arrive here from Europe, it was a rare thing for fifty to survive the first year; that of those fifty, half would be in hospital, and not ten of the rest in perfect health: the pale and feeble wretches whom we saw crawling about with a musket, which they were scarcely able to carry, inclined us to believe that it was true.

In such a climate, amid the disease-laden air, it is not surprising that the inhabitants acquired a macabre indifference to death: "when an aquaintance is said to be dead, the common reply is, 'Well, he owed me nothing,' or, 'I must get my money off his executors.' "

In this death-trap harbour, the Admiralty unconcernedly left the warrant officers of H.M.S. *Falmouth* to rot. The ship had been condemned at Batavia, on its way home from Manila and the crew, with the exception of the warrant officers, returned to England. For many years they sent petitions to the Admiralty pleading to be allowed home, but, luckily for them, the Dutch, eventually tired of the situation and about six months before *Endeavour's* arrival, sold the vessel by public auction and sent the officers home in one of their own ships.

Here, too, slaves were sold. Their price was from "ten to twenty pounds sterling; but girls, if they have beauty, sometimes fetch a hundred." The government only imposed one restriction on the owners of these poor wretches — they must not kill them. If therefore a slave had to be punished, an owner would, as a safety precaution, apply to a specially appointed officer to inflict the punishment. He in turn owned several of the strongest, most brutish male slaves money could buy, trained exclusively to inflict horrible punishments, "bred up to the business," says Cook. The slave owners paid six shillings and eight pence for the hire of these monsters. Naturally enough, the commonest criminals were runaway slaves, and for this they were beaten with a ghastly weapon, a thick piece of bamboo split down many times, called a rattan. It was almost a handful of knives and "fetched blood at every stroke." The male slaves were lashed to their master's door and beaten in public, and it was no uncommon sight for *Endeavour's* men to see the poor wretches being ferociously flogged, their backs like raw beefsteaks. The women were beaten indoors.

The criminal code for the free natives of the country was almost as severe as that of the slaves. "They are hanged, and broken at the wheel and even impaled alive, without mercy." But for the Europeans, however frightful their crimes, there existed a yawning gap between their treatment and that of the slaves: "they were always indulged with an opportunity of escaping before being brought to trial." Once within the clutches of the law, they were sent to Edam, a Dutch devil's island, where

> they transport all Europeans who have been found guilty of crimes not worthy of death: some are sentenced to remain there ninety nine years, some forty, some twenty, some less, in proportion to their offences; and, during their banishment, they are employed as slaves in making ropes and other drudgery.

Among people living in such unhealthy conditions, ground down by merciless laws, passions, when roused, ran high and to extremes. Knife duels and murders were commonplace; slaves, even free citizens, were driven frantic by jealousies, hate, and the gross inequalities of the system of government.

> The practice that is called "running amok" has prevailed amongst these people for time immemorial; one of the officers, whose business it is to apprehend such people, told us that there was scarcely a week in which he was not called upon to take one of them into custody.

Cook passed on the warning to his men, never to stand

in the way of these opium-crazed madmen, for that was always the first move: they would brood over their wrongs till, drunk on opium, they murdered their oppressor, then rushed into the street with a weapon in hand, "frantic and foaming at the mouth," and murder whoever attempted to arrest them. Mostly they were slaves, who were subject to the worst insults and least able to obtain legal redress.

> If the officer takes one of these "amoks" alive, his reward is very considerable, but if he kills him, nothing is added to his usual pay: yet such is the fury of their desperation, that three out of four are of necessity destroyed in the attempt to secure them, though the officers are provided with instruments like large tongs or pincers, to lay hold of them without coming within the reach of their weapon. Those who happen to be taken alive are generally wounded, but they are always broken alive upon the wheel: and if the physician who is appointed to examine their wounds, thinks them likely to be mortal, the punishment is inflicted immediately, and the place of execution is generally the spot where the first murder was committed.

On *Endeavour's* arrival at Batavia she had been a badly battered, scarcely seaworthy vessel, but within her rotting timbers she contained a healthy ship's company. Now, as the days lengthened into weeks, the position was reversed. Under the personal supervision of Cook and the good work of the Dutch shipwrights, "the bottom of the ship was thoroughly repaired, and very much to my satisfaction . . . there is not a marine yard in the world where a ship can be repaired with more diligence and skill. . . ." The scars and wounds of the Yorkshire coal boat were healed while the clammy deathlike hand of tropical disease descended on the ship's company, unfought and unchallenged. The pages of Cook's journal at this time are tragic. It is easy to detect the hopelessness he experienced, every fibre of him a fighter unable to help his dying men.

> Our distress was now very great: our danger was not such as we could surmount by any efforts of our own; courage, skill and diligence were all equally ineffectual, and death was every day making advances upon us, where we could neither resist nor fly.

With the ship laid up in dock, all except the smallest maintenance party were moved ashore, the men to tents and the officers and gentlemen into hotels, which were bad, dirty, expensive for those days ("nine shillings sterling a-day for each"), and served ill-cooked, unclean food. At first Tupia, who had been ill on their arrival, recovered a little at all the wondrous new sights he and his servant Tayeto were seeing for the first time, "dancing along the streets in a kind of ecstasy." But the unhealthiness of the climate soon began to tell on the two Polynesians, who grew progressively worse. Of the crew, "there were not more than ten that were able to do their duty," and the sick of necessity were left to the mercy of Malay servants, so idle that they would not lift a hand to give the dying men water. Dr. Solander was gravely ill and Banks suffering from fits "so violent as to deprive him of his senses while they lasted, and leave him so weak he was scarcely able to crawl down stairs." Conditions were so bad in the hotel that they were forced to rent a house farther inland. To make matters worse Mr. Monkhouse, the surgeon,

> a sensible, skillful man, fell the first sacrific to this fatal country, a loss which was greatly aggravated by our situation . . . on the ninth, we lost our poor native boy Tayeto, and Tupia was so much affected, that it was doubted whether he would survive to the next day.

He just lasted the twenty-four hours, "sinking at once after the loss of the boy, whom he loved with the tenderness of a parent." The death of Tupia affected them all deeply. The kindly, aristocratic Tahitan priest; the proud descendant of a lost and forgotten race whose beginnings fade into the misty obscurity of long forgotten, never recorded history. Tupia, whose gentle manners soothed the fears of Maori boys; Tupia, who gallantly called on his gods for rain when it was already pouring, and prophesied the coming of wind as the sails tautened in a stiff gale. He was loved and respected by every man aboard, a stranger among these roughened, coarse-mouthed English seamen. Often they had smiled at him, but the inherent gentle courteousness of the man had won him the affection of them all. Now he was dead.

Cook, too, who rightly considered himself as tough as a brewer's dray horse, fell ill, but refused to give in and forced himself back to health. Only one man of the whole ship's company remained in normal health, the sailmaker, truly an ancient mariner — "between seventy and eighty years of age," with a constitution like well-cured cowhide — ever to have survived life at sea in those days to such a ripe old age. "And it is remarkable," says Cook, "that this old man, during our stay at this place, was constantly drunk every day." It was fortunate as well as remarkable for that crusty old salt.

In all, they buried seven of their comrades at Batavia — the surgeon, three seamen, a servant, Tupia and Tayeto, his boy. It was small comfort to be told by the Governor that they had been lucky to lose so few.

But their actual losses at Batavia were not a true picture of their real state, for when they finally weighed anchor on the 27th of December and sailed west for Cape Town, the ship was like a floating hospital. Between decks, the sick tossed and sweated in the last throes of dysentery and malaria; the ship stank of death; there were too few men fit to work the ship and attend adequately to the sick. "At this time the number of sick amounted to forty, and the rest of the ship's company were in a very feeble condition." Cook had to sail, even with his crew in such bad shape, for to have remained longer at Batavia — the white man's grave of the East — would have been fatal.

The passage from Batavia to Cape Town took just under three months: months of horror and death, of despondency and even madness. It became an almost nightly routine to gather on the upper deck, listening sadly to the burial service, waiting tensely for the final splash as another comrade was flung overboard. The situation demanded from Cook an iron grip on his crew, for the men were nearly hysterical as they wandered among the sick and dying. One sailor, apparently in reasonable health, woke up one morning with a stomach ache. Certain his turn had come, he rushed screaming on deck, "I have got the gripes, I have got the gripes . . . I shall die, I shall die!" Overcome with fright he threw a fit, after which he was perfectly all right.

None were spared:

> the seeds of disease which we had received at Batavia began to appear with the most threatening symptoms in dysentery and slow fevers. Lest the water should have any share in our sickness, we purified it with lime and we washed all parts of the ship between decks with vinegar, as a remedy against infection. Mr. Banks was amongst the sick, and for some time there was no hope of his life. We were very soon in a most deplorable situation; the ship was nothing better than a hospital, in which those that were able to go about were too few to attend to the sick, who were confined in their hammocks; and we had almost every night a dead body to commit to the sea. In the course of about six weeks, we buried Mr. Sporing, a gentleman who was in Mr. Banks' retinue; Mr. Parkinson, natural history painter; Mr. Green, the astronomer [and Cook's especial friend], the boatswain, the carpenter and his mate; Mr. Monkhouse, the midshipman who had fothered the ship after she had been stranded on the coast of Australia; our old jolly sailmaker and his assistant, the ship's cook, the corporal of the marines, two of the carpenter's crew, a midshipman and nine seamen; in all three and twenty persons, besides the seven that we buried at Batavia.

After eleven days sailing in hot, sultry weather, making

life for the fevered sick almost unendurable, they picked up the southeast trade wind and arrived at Cape Town on the 15th of March. Cook's first concern was to get the sick ashore. At last some improvement was evident among the men. Though they had suffered terribly, their casualties were really not great for the time they had been at sea. While they lay at the Cape an Indiaman sailed for England which had been away barely a year, yet she had lost by "sickness between thirty and forty men and when she left the Cape had many in a helpless condition with the scurvy . . . our sufferings therefore, were comparatively light considering that we had been away near three times as long."

For a month they lingered there, taking in the necessary stores to get them home and doing essential repairs. Cook was not impressed by South Africa, though he thought the Dutch were making the best of a bad job; "no country we have seen affords so barren a prospect as this." But the Dutch women pleased him:

> . . . in general they are very handsome; they have fine clear skins and a bloom of colour that indicates a purity of condition and high health. They make the best wives in the world, both as mistress of a family and mother; and there is scarcely a house that does not swarm with children.

Extra crew were embarked to help them on the homeward voyage, the sick "were taken aboard, several of whom were in a dangerous state," and on the 14th of April they sailed for home. Yet death still remained with them, for a few days later, "we lost our Master, Mr. Robert Molineux, a young man of good parts, but unhappily given up to intemperance, which brought on the disorder that put an end to his life."

A last brief stop at St. Helena, then in company with twelve other ships and a British man-of-war, they sailed for England on the last long weary leg of the voyage. But *Endeavour* was now in a bad way, nearly beyond repair, for the work that had been done at the Cape was no more than a temporary stopgap and Cook was glad of the company of other ships. "Our riggings and sails were now become so bad, that something was giving way every day." Never a fast ship and now hindered by half-rotten equipment, it was clear, six days after leaving St. Helena, that *Endeavour* would not be able to keep up with the other vessels. The Captain realized that the last few thousand miles would have to be battled out alone, as had the rest of the voyage round the world.

On the evening of the 9th of May, Cook decided that the next day he would ask the captain of the British man-of-war to take into his possession for delivery to the Admiralty "a box containing the common logbooks of the ship and the journals of some of the officers." He accompanied these with a letter, dated *"Endeavour Bark,* 9th May, 1771," and made mention of the deplorable sickness on board in the following terms:

> That uninterrupted state of health we had all along enjoyed was soon after our arrival at Batavia succeeded by a general sickness which delayed us so much, that it was 26th December before we were able to leave this place. We were fortunate enough to lose but few men at

> Batavia, but in our passage from thence to the Cape of Good Hope we had twenty-three men died . . . all, or most of them, of the bloody flux. The fatal disorder reigned in the ship with such obstinacy that medicine, however skillfully administered, had not the least effect.

The next morning, "perceiving that we sailed much heavier than any other ship," Cook handed over his precious parcel to Captain Elliot of the British man-of-war.

For another twelve days they hung on to the tail of the convoy: then as day broke over the grey heaving swell of the Atlantic on the morning of the 23rd of May, "there was not one of the ships in sight." Below decks death snatched her last victim; the last of a tragically long list of splendid seamen who should have lived to tell the tale. "About one o'clock in the afternoon died our First Lieutenant, Mr. Hicks, and in the evening we committed his body to the sea with the usual ceremonies." It was consumption that killed him, he had embarked on that world voyage suffering from it; "it may truly be said he was dying during the whole voyage, though his decline was very gradual till we came to Batavia." The death of Hicks brought the total up to thirty-eight. *Endeavour* had sailed with a complement of ninety-four officers, passengers, and men. Up to their arrival at Batavia, only eight men were lost, mostly through unavoidable accidents. An astoundingly brilliant performance on Cook's part, and the whole merit for it must go to him. True, some of the medicines and methods he used were not his own inventions, but if they were available to him, then obviously they were at the disposal of all other British sea captains, but they never troubled to employ them, for we know that it was commonplace for ships to lose fifty per cent of their crews in a twelve-month, not three years, the time Cook had been away. Of the eleven civilians, four were left, and in the dreadful last months which included Batavia, thirty men died, so that of the original ninety-four persons aboard, fifty-six lived to see England again. It was a sad end to a splendid voyage, but still immeasurably better than any previous expedition.

It took the game little ship a month to complete the passage from St. Helena to England, probably for the Captain the most worrying month of the voyage, with his ship almost breaking up under him. It is easy to imagine the terrific excitement aboard as they approached home, after nearly three years of being away, all straining their eyes for a first glimpse of the old country. On the 10th of June, 1771, the sharp eyes of Nicholas Young, the same boy who had first sighted New Zealand, spotted the Lizard. They were home.

> On the 11th we ran up the channel; at six in the morning of the 12th we passed Beachy Head; at noon we were abreast of Dover, and about three came to an anchor in the Downs and went ashore at Deal.

Perhaps as they ran into harbour it was possible to detect a faraway look in some of their eyes, straying back over the thousands of tossing miles of ocean they had crossed; back to the island paradise of Tahiti and the lovely, dusky girls they had left behind, "Sometimes sparkling with fire and sometimes melting with softness."

Principal Sources
Index

PRINCIPAL SOURCES

A JOURNAL *of a Voyage round the World in the "Endeavour," 1771, published in Hawkesworth's Voyages, 1773. Describing his discoveries and adventures in Tierra del Fuego, Tahiti, New Zealand, Van Dieman's Land and Australia . . . Partly narrated by the great navigator himself; partly compiled from his notes and journals, and the papers of J. Banks by Dr. Hawkesworth.*

Captain Cook's Voyages of Discovery, edited by John Barrow, F.R.S., F.S.A., Secretary to the Admiralty. First published 1860, republished for Everyman's Library, London, J. M. Dent and Sons, Ltd., 1906.

Cook and the Opening of the Pacific, by James A. Williamson, edited by A. L. Rowse. London: Hodder and Stoughton, Ltd., 1946, for the English University Press.

The British Fleet, by Commander C. N. Robinson, R.N. London: George Bell and Sons, 1894.

Captain Cook, by Christopher Lloyd, M.A., F.R.Hist.S. London: Faber and Faber, 1952.

The Mutiny and Piratical Seizure of H.M.S. Bounty, by Sir John Barrow with an introduction by Admiral Sir Cyprian Bridge, G.C.B. First published in 1831, and republished by the Oxford University Press.

Further accounts of the life of Captain Cook, from which the background has been built up, include:

The Exploration of the Pacific, by J. C. Beaglehole (London, 1934).

Life of Captain Cook, by Hugh Carrington (London, 1939).

Captain James Cook, by Sir Joseph Carruthers (London, 1930).

Captain Cook, by Lieutenant-Commander R. T. Gould (London, 1935).

History of Geographical Discovery in the Seventeenth and Eighteenth Centuries, by Edward Heawood (Cambridge, 1912).

Captain James Cook, by Rear-Admiral J. R. Muir, Surg. (London, 1939).

Captain Cook's Journal . . . Made in H.M. Bark "Endeavour," by Captain W. J. L. Wharton (London, 1893).

The Discovery of Australia, by G. Arnold Wood (London, 1922).

The Life of Captain James Cook, by A. Kippis, D.D., F.R.S. (1788).

Captain Cook, by Walter Besant (1889).

Captain James Cook, the Circumnavigator, by Arthur Kitson (1907).

Article on Cook in the *DNB* by Sir J. K. Laughton.

Documents, plans, and photographs giving particulars of the *Endeavour* found in: *The Mariner's Mirror,* Vol. XIX, No. 3 (July 1933), and *H.M. Bark Endeavour,* by C. Knight.

A study of letters and Cook's journal at the Public Record Office, London.

The good fortune to follow closely in the tracks of Cook's first voyage with the British Pacific Fleet in 1944.

INDEX